YASIR ARAFAT

MENACHEM BEGIN

TONY BLAIR

GEORGE W. BUSH

JIMMY CARTER

FIDEL CASTRO

VICENTE FOX

SADDAM HUSSEIN

HAMID KARZAI

KIM IL SUNG AND KIM JONG IL

HOSNI MUBARAK

PERVEZ MUSHARRAF

VLADIMIR PUTIN

MOHAMMED REZA PAHLAVI

ANWAR SADAT

THE SAUDI ROYAL FAMILY

GERHARD SCHROEDER

ARIEL SHARON

Kim Il Sung
and
Kim Jong Il

Rachel A. Koestler-Grack

CHELSEA HOUSE
PUBLISHERS
A Haights Cross Communications ✦ Company

Philadelphia

CHELSEA HOUSE PUBLISHERS

V.P., NEW PRODUCT DEVELOPMENT Sally Cheney
DIRECTOR OF PRODUCTION Kim Shinners
CREATIVE MANAGER Takeshi Takahashi
MANUFACTURING MANAGER Diann Grasse

Staff for KIM IL SUNG AND KIM JONG IL

EXECUTIVE EDITOR Lee Marcott
SENIOR EDITOR Tara Koellhoffer
PRODUCTION EDITOR Megan Emery
PICTURE RESEARCH 21st Century Publishing and Communications, Inc.
SERIES AND COVER DESIGNER Takeshi Takahashi
LAYOUT 21st Century Publishing and Communications, Inc.

A Haights Cross Communications ⌖ Company

http://www.chelseahouse.com

First Printing

1 3 5 7 9 8 6 4 2

Library of Congress Cataloging-in-Publication Data

Koestler-Grack, Rachel A., 1973–
   Kim Il Sung and Kim Jong Il / by Rachel A. Koestler-Grack.
      p. cm.—(Major world leaders)
Summary: A biography of two Korean leaders, father and son, whose policies of self-reliance and self-defense are intended to lead to their primary goal—a united Korea.
Includes bibliographical references and index.
   ISBN 0-7910-7648-2
   1. Kim, Il-sæong, 1912– —Juvenile literature. 2. Kim, Chæong-il, 1942– —Juvenile literature. 3. Heads of state—Korea (North)—Biography—Juvenile literature. 4. Korea (North)—Politics and government. [1. Kim, Il-sæong, 1912– 2. Kim, Chæong-il, 1942– 3. Heads of state—Korea (North) 4. Korea (North)—Politics and government.] I. Title. II. Series.
DS934.6.K5K64 2003
951.9304'3'0922—dc21

                                                            2003013688

TABLE OF CONTENTS

On Leadership

Arthur M. Schlesinger, jr.

Leadership, it may be said, is really what makes the world go round. Love no doubt smoothes the passage; but love is a private transaction between consenting adults. Leadership is a public transaction with history. The idea of leadership affirms the capacity of individuals to move, inspire, and mobilize masses of people so that they act together in pursuit of an end. Sometimes leadership serves good purposes, sometimes bad; but whether the end is benign or evil, great leaders are those men and women who leave their personal stamp on history.

Now, the very concept of leadership implies the proposition that individuals can make a difference. This proposition has never been universally accepted. From classical times to the present day, eminent thinkers have regarded individuals as no more than the agents and pawns of larger forces, whether the gods and goddesses of the ancient world or, in the modern era, race, class, nation, the dialectic, the will of the people, the spirit of the times, history itself. Against such forces, the individual dwindles into insignificance.

So contends the thesis of historical determinism. Tolstoy's great novel *War and Peace* offers a famous statement of the case. Why, Tolstoy asked, did millions of men in the Napoleonic Wars, denying their human feelings and their common sense, move back and forth across Europe slaughtering their fellows? "The war," Tolstoy answered, "was bound to happen simply because it was bound to happen." All prior history determined it. As for leaders, they, Tolstoy said, "are but the labels that serve to give a name to an end and, like labels, they have the least possible connection with the event." The greater the leader, "the more conspicuous the inevitability and the predestination of every act he commits." The leader, said Tolstoy, is "the slave of history."

Determinism takes many forms. Marxism is the determinism of class. Nazism the determinism of race. But the idea of men and women as the slaves of history runs athwart the deepest human instincts. Rigid determinism abolishes the idea of human freedom—the assumption of free choice that underlies every move we make, every word we speak, every thought we think. It abolishes the idea of human responsibility, since it is manifestly unfair to reward or punish people for actions that are by definition beyond their control. No one can live consistently by any deterministic creed. The Marxist states prove this themselves by their extreme susceptibility to the cult of leadership.

More than that, history refutes the idea that individuals make no difference. In December 1931 a British politician crossing Fifth Avenue in New York City between 76th and 77th Streets around 10:30 P.M. looked in the wrong direction and was knocked down by an automobile— a moment, he later recalled, of a man aghast, a world aglare: "I do not understand why I was not broken like an eggshell or squashed like a gooseberry." Fourteen months later an American politician, sitting in an open car in Miami, Florida, was fired on by an assassin; the man beside him was hit. Those who believe that individuals make no difference to history might well ponder whether the next two decades would have been the same had Mario Constasino's car killed Winston Churchill in 1931 and Giuseppe Zangara's bullet killed Franklin Roosevelt in 1933. Suppose, in addition, that Lenin had died of typhus in Siberia in 1895 and that Hitler had been killed on the Western Front in 1916. What would the 20th century have looked like now?

For better or for worse, individuals do make a difference. "The notion that a people can run itself and its affairs anonymously," wrote the philosopher William James, "is now well known to be the silliest of absurdities. Mankind does nothing save through initiatives on the part of inventors, great or small, and imitation by the rest of us—these are the sole factors in human progress. Individuals of genius show the way, and set the patterns, which common people then adopt and follow."

Leadership, James suggests, means leadership in thought as well as in action. In the long run, leaders in thought may well make the greater difference to the world. "The ideas of economists and political philosophers, both when they are right and when they are wrong," wrote John Maynard Keynes, "are more powerful than is commonly understood. Indeed the world is ruled by little else. Practical men, who believe themselves to be quite exempt from any intellectual influences, are usually the slaves of some defunct economist. . . . The power of vested interests is vastly exaggerated compared with the gradual encroachment of ideas."

But, as Woodrow Wilson once said, "Those only are leaders of men, in the general eye, who lead in action. . . . It is at their hands that new thought gets its translation into the crude language of deeds." Leaders in thought often invent in solitude and obscurity, leaving to later generations the tasks of imitation. Leaders in action—the leaders portrayed in this series—have to be effective in their own time.

And they cannot be effective by themselves. They must act in response to the rhythms of their age. Their genius must be adapted, in a phrase from William James, "to the receptivities of the moment." Leaders are useless without followers. "There goes the mob," said the French politician, hearing a clamor in the streets. "I am their leader. I must follow them." Great leaders turn the inchoate emotions of the mob to purposes of their own. They seize on the opportunities of their time, the hopes, fears, frustrations, crises, potentialities. They succeed when events have prepared the way for them, when the community is awaiting to be aroused, when they can provide the clarifying and organizing ideas. Leadership completes the circuit between the individual and the mass and thereby alters history.

It may alter history for better or for worse. Leaders have been responsible for the most extravagant follies and most monstrous crimes that have beset suffering humanity. They have also been vital in such gains as humanity has made in individual freedom, religious and racial tolerance, social justice, and respect for human rights.

There is no sure way to tell in advance who is going to lead for good and who for evil. But a glance at the gallery of men and women in MAJOR WORLD LEADERS suggests some useful tests.

One test is this: Do leaders lead by force or by persuasion? By command or by consent? Through most of history leadership was exercised by the divine right of authority. The duty of followers was to defer and to obey. "Theirs not to reason why/Theirs but to do and die." On occasion, as with the so-called enlightened despots of the 18th century in Europe, absolutist leadership was animated by humane purposes. More often, absolutism nourished the passion for domination, land, gold, and conquest and resulted in tyranny.

The great revolution of modern times has been the revolution of equality. "Perhaps no form of government," wrote the British historian James Bryce in his study of the United States, *The American Commonwealth,* "needs great leaders so much as democracy." The idea that all people should be equal in their legal condition has undermined the old structure of authority, hierarchy, and deference. The revolution of equality has had two contrary effects on the nature of leadership. For equality, as Alexis de Tocqueville pointed out in his great study *Democracy in America*, might mean equality in servitude as well as equality in freedom.

"I know of only two methods of establishing equality in the political world," Tocqueville wrote. "Rights must be given to every citizen, or none at all to anyone . . . save one, who is the master of all." There was no middle ground "between the sovereignty of all and the absolute power of one man." In his astonishing prediction of 20th-century totalitarian dictatorship, Tocqueville explained how the revolution of equality could lead to the *Führerprinzip* and more terrible absolutism than the world had ever known.

But when rights are given to every citizen and the sovereignty of all is established, the problem of leadership takes a new form, becomes more exacting than ever before. It is easy to issue commands and enforce them by the rope and the stake, the concentration camp and the *gulag*. It is much harder to use argument and achievement to overcome opposition and win consent. The Founding Fathers of the United States understood the difficulty. They believed that history had given them the opportunity to decide, as Alexander Hamilton wrote in the first Federalist Paper, whether men are indeed capable of basing government on "reflection and choice, or whether they are forever destined to depend . . . on accident and force."

Government by reflection and choice called for a new style of leadership and a new quality of followership. It required leaders to be responsive to popular concerns, and it required followers to be active and informed participants in the process. Democracy does not eliminate emotion from politics; sometimes it fosters demagoguery; but it is confident that, as the greatest of democratic leaders put it, you cannot fool all of the people all of the time. It measures leadership by results and retires those who overreach or falter or fail.

It is true that in the long run despots are measured by results too. But they can postpone the day of judgment, sometimes indefinitely, and in the meantime they can do infinite harm. It is also true that democracy is no guarantee of virtue and intelligence in government, for the voice of the people is not necessarily the voice of God. But democracy, by assuring the right of opposition, offers built-in resistance to the evils inherent in absolutism. As the theologian Reinhold Niebuhr summed it up, "Man's capacity for justice makes democracy possible, but man's inclination to justice makes democracy necessary."

A second test for leadership is the end for which power is sought. When leaders have as their goal the supremacy of a master race or the promotion of totalitarian revolution or the acquisition and exploitation of colonies or the protection of greed and privilege or the preservation of personal power, it is likely that their leadership will do little to advance the cause of humanity. When their goal is the abolition of slavery, the liberation of women, the enlargement of opportunity for the poor and powerless, the extension of equal rights to racial minorities, the defense of the freedoms of expression and opposition, it is likely that their leadership will increase the sum of human liberty and welfare.

Leaders have done great harm to the world. They have also conferred great benefits. You will find both sorts in this series. Even "good" leaders must be regarded with a certain wariness. Leaders are not demigods; they put on their trousers one leg after another just like ordinary mortals. No leader is infallible, and every leader needs to be reminded of this at regular intervals. Irreverence irritates leaders but is their salvation. Unquestioning submission corrupts leaders and demeans followers. Making a cult of a leader is always a mistake. Fortunately hero worship generates its own antidote. "Every hero," said Emerson, "becomes a bore at last."

The signal benefit the great leaders confer is to embolden the rest of us to live according to our own best selves, to be active, insistent, and resolute in affirming our own sense of things. For great leaders attest to the reality of human freedom against the supposed inevitabilities of history. And they attest to the wisdom and power that may lie within the most unlikely of us, which is why Abraham Lincoln remains the supreme example of great leadership. A great leader, said Emerson, exhibits new possibilities to all humanity. "We feed on genius. . . . Great men exist that there may be greater men."

Great leaders, in short, justify themselves by emancipating and empowering their followers. So humanity struggles to master its destiny, remembering with Alexis de Tocqueville: "It is true that around every man a fatal circle is traced beyond which he cannot pass; but within the wide verge of that circle he is powerful and free; as it is with man, so with communities." ■

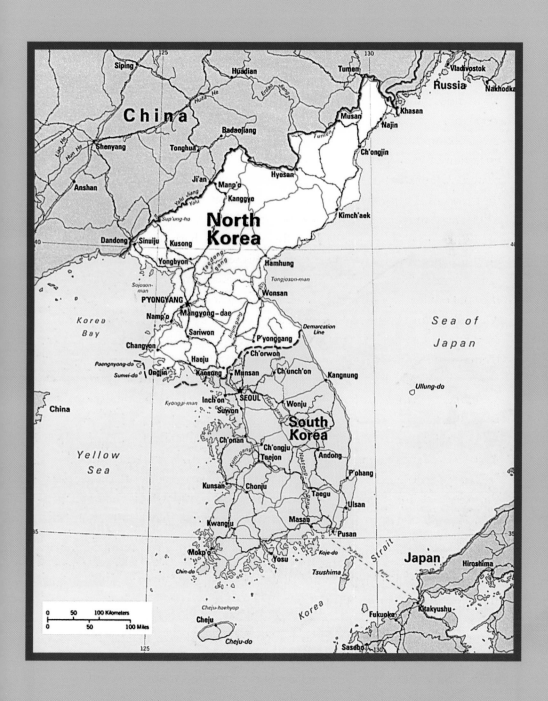

1

Father and Son Enjoy the Noise

On Sunday, March 2, 2003, a U.S. reconnaissance plane flew over the Sea of Japan, about 150 miles (241 kilometers) off the coast of North Korea. The RC-135 reconnaissance plane left mid-morning on a routine mission in international airspace. At 10:48 A.M., four North Korean fighter jets closed in on the plane. Two MiG-29 fighters flew at equal altitude on either side of the reconnaissance plane, wing-tip to wing-tip. The other two fighters remained at the rear. At times, the armed fighters came within 50 feet (15 meters) of the aircraft. During the engagement, at least one of the North Korean fighters may have locked on to the reconnaissance jet with its fire-support radar. After 22 minutes of shadowing, the fighters disengaged, and the American airplane safely landed at Kadena Air Base in Japan.

This incident was the first direct hostile act that North Korea

North Korean leader Kim Jong Il, center, being briefed during a military exercise at an undisclosed location. A series of events in early 2003 has placed North Korea on a collision course with the United States.

had made toward the United States since 1969. North Korea claimed the plane had crossed into its airspace, but the aircraft was well outside Korean boundaries. However, the interception of the reconnaissance plane was just one instance in a series of events that currently pose a threat of war in Korea. In February 2003, the North Koreans reactivated their nuclear reactors, which had been shut down since 1994. The North Korean leader Kim Jong Il threatened to annul the 1953 Korean War armistice and take military action against South Korea. On February 24, not quite a week before the interception of the American plane, North Korea flexed its muscles by firing a missile into the Sea of Japan.

Kim Jong Il may be taunting the United States into a fight over an issue that has been the primary cause for unrest in

Korea since its people were liberated from Japan in 1945. He hopes to achieve the goal that his father, Kim Il Sung, spent his lifetime trying to accomplish—a united Korea. Like his father, he will make a little noise about it. Over the years, North Korean leaders have accused the United States of trying to invade the North. In peace talks with the South, North Koreans repeatedly encouraged the South to break off relations with the United States. If the United States had not intervened, North Korea would have won the Korean War and united the country by force. In many ways, North Korea sees the United States as its primary roadblock to reunification.

Korea has a long history of unrest. Over 2,000 years of recorded history, Korea has experienced 900 years of invasions, both large and small. It has endured five major eras of foreign occupation, by forces that included China, the Mongols, and Japan. After World War II, Korea was occupied by the Soviet Union in the north and the United States in the south. When the Soviet occupational authorities withdrew, North Korean leader Kim Il Sung worked to build an independent socialist state. To aid in this endeavor, Kim formed strong alliances with the two countries that share Korea's northern border—the Soviet Union and China. Kim continually denounced U.S. influence in South Korea, calling America an imperialist country.

North Korea's ill feelings toward the United States stem back to pre-Japanese occupation. In 1882, Korea signed a treaty with the United States. In the agreement, the United States promised to be a trustworthy ally to Korea in the event of an external threat. In 1904, Russia and Japan fought the Russo-Japanese War over control of Korea. The Japanese won a surprising victory, which placed them in a strong position to occupy Korea. In 1905, William Howard Taft, then the U.S. secretary of state, made a secret agreement with the Japanese foreign minister. In exchange for assurances that Japan would not interfere with U.S. colonial interests in the Philippines, the United States approved Japan's domination of Korea. The agreement violated the U.S. promise to Korea and brought ghastly consequences for the people of Korea. Japan quickly moved in, occupying Korea in 1905 and claiming it as a Japanese possession five years later. From 1910 until World War II (1939–1945), Japan governed Korea as a brutal colonial tyrant.

Out of the years of cruel Japanese rule grew a strong fighter. Kim Il Sung watched his father and other patriots devote their lives to the fight for Korean independence. When his father finally sacrificed his life, Kim picked up his weapons and joined the crusade. As a guerrilla fighter, he earned the respect and admiration of his comrades-in-arms. After liberation, Kim continued to devote his life to restoring Korea to its original state. He helped form a lasting socialist government, and passed his legacy on to his son, Kim Jong Il. Their policies of self-reliance and self-defense have helped the small country of North Korea become strong enough to capture the attention of the entire world.

2

Early Years of Japanese Rule

On April 15, 1912, Kim Il Sung was born in his family's home in the village of Mangyong-dae near Pyongyang, Korea. He was the first of three boys. Kim's mother, Kang Bang Suk, and father, Kim Hyong Jik, gave him the name Kim Sung Ju. Mangyong-dae was a beautiful village surrounded by green mountains from which one could look down on the breathtaking landscape of the Taedong River.

Many generations of Kim's family had lived in Mangyong-dae. His great-great-grandfather came to northern Korea from Chun-ju in the North Chul-ra Province. He hoped to find a better life for himself and his family. Years later, in 1860, Kim's great-grandfather Kim Ung Woo settled in Mangyong-dae. Like many other Koreans, Kim Ung Woo made a living through farming. He also worked as the caretaker of a rich landowner's ancestral burial ground near Mangyong-dae. So it was that Kim's grandfather and father also became farmers of small patches of land in Mangyong-dae.

When Kim's father was young, he learned the 1,000-character prose of the Korean language from a village scholar. Kim Hyong Jik was eager to gain a higher education at formal schools, however. He wanted to become a medical doctor. In the late 1800s, many families could not afford an education. In order for Kim Hyong Jik to attend school, the whole family worked extra jobs to contribute to the cost. Kim Hyong Jik's wife collected clams from the Sunwha River and sold them on the village streets, his father sold sweet melons from his garden, and his mother and 15-year-old brother worked the fields. Kim Hyong Jik also worked extra hours at the school's experimental farm after classes. He then studied at the school library for several hours and walked over seven miles (12 kilometers) back home. When he got home, he had only two hours' sleep before he rose for breakfast and another grueling day.

Despite their hard work, Kim's family often had little to eat. Some days they could not even afford a small bowl of thin rice gruel. They sometimes ate unprocessed grains instead. These grains usually were fed to the animals. Kim later said, "I still recall how much trouble I had swallowing those coarse hard-to-digest grains." Fruits and meats were too expensive for Kim's family to afford.

Poverty was not the only hardship Kim's family endured. Before Kim was born, Korea fell under Japanese rule. The Japanese emperor controlled Korea under an annexation agreement. Under the terms laid out in this document, Korean leaders signed control of the country to the Japanese governor-general. Japanese leaders disbanded all Korean political and scholastic organizations. Even schoolteachers

An image of Japanese troops occupying Seoul, Korea, in 1904. As a child, Kim Il Sung learned to hate the Japanese colonizers. Much of his early life was influenced by the struggle for Korean independence.

wore uniforms and carried samurai swords. Koreans lived in fear of the Japanese secret police, who terrorized the people. The Japanese took away the Korean people's freedom of press, freedom to hold meetings, freedom to march, and many other rights. By the time he was five years old, Kim learned to detest the Japanese colonists. Like the rest of his family, he believed the Koreans should fight to regain their independence.

As soon as Kim was old enough to understand, his father began to lecture him about the importance of patriotism. His father told him to think *ji-won*, which means "righteous aspirations." *Ji-won* stands for grand ideas for doing good. Righteous aspirations were not about achieving worldly fame, riches, and power, but rather receiving satisfaction and happiness from fighting for Korea. Kim's father taught him that patriotism would lead a person to fight year after year, generation after generation, for however long it would take to liberate Korea.

Many Koreans refused to live compliantly under Japanese rule. They formed secret organizations, held resistance meetings, and engaged in independent fights. Many patriots joined Chinese guerrilla fighters and participated in surprise attacks on the Japanese. When Kim was six years old, his father left home during the winter to fight with Chinese guerrillas farther north. Kim hoped his father would make a quick return, but as winter stretched into spring, Kim's father had not yet come home.

THE MARCH FIRST MOVEMENT

On March 1, 1919, all the pent-up anger and oppression felt by the Korean people exploded in the March First Movement. At noon, church bells throughout the city of Pyongyang rang out in unison. Several thousand students and citizens gathered at Sung-duk Girls' School at Jang-dae-jae. A declaration of independence was read aloud on the front yard, proclaiming

Korea a free nation. The crowd shouted, "Long live Korean independence! Out with the Japanese and their army!" Thousands more joined the rally.

In Mangyong-dae, Kim lined up with his family and hundreds of villagers and marched to Pyongyang. Along the way, Koreans dropped their rakes and shovels in the fields and joined the march. By the time they reached the city, the crowd of marchers had grown to several thousand. Six-year-old Kim marched with holes in the bottoms of his shoes, shouting, "Long live Korean independence!"

In Pyongyang, the Korean protesters joined together and marched to the Botong Gate of the Pyongyang Castle. This building was the center of military defense in Korea. Japanese troops and the police charged the protesters to stop the march. They fired shots into the crowd and slashed their swords at random marchers. Kim saw many Koreans fall to the ground, bleeding to death. It was the first time he had ever witnessed people killing people. Despite the Japanese resistance, the Korean protesters marched on, fighting with their bare hands.

After sunset, villagers from Mangyong-dae withdrew to Mangyong Peak and held a rally at its summit. They lit torches, sounded bugles, beat drums and metal pans, and cried out for independence. The summit rally lasted for several days.

News about the March First Movement spread quickly through Korea. In Seoul, another march began, this time with several hundred thousand people. Again, Japanese soldiers opened fire on the marchers. The soldiers showed no discrimination in their attacks. According to Kim Il Sung's memoirs (which historians believe may not be completely accurate), the Japanese slashed off the hands of young schoolgirls who marched with the Korean flag held high. The people's determination was unshaken, though. The girls picked up the flags with their other hands and continued marching. For about two months, the entire Korean Peninsula sounded with shouts of independence.

The March First Movement did not end in victory for the Korean people. The leaders of the movement insisted on nonviolent protests. Their marches accomplished little for the people. The Japanese had fought three major wars to gain control of Korea. They were not about to be pushed easily out of the country. But the Korean people desired action. They were willing to fight and die for their independence. The people learned that what they needed was effective revolutionary leadership and the use of the right tactics and strategies. For Kim, the March First Movement changed his life forever. He later recalled, "[It] placed me in the rank of the people and left an image on my eyes of the true nature of the Korean people. Whenever I hear the echo of the March First hurrahs in my mind's ears, I feel so proud of the Korean people's unbending determination and heroism."

FORCED TO MOVE

Kim's seventh birthday came without any word from his father. He found it difficult to smile and celebrate through his worries. A few months after Kim's birthday, a letter from his father finally arrived. Along with the letter, Kim's father sent him a calligraphy set of a brush and ink, made in China. Kim's father wanted Kim to be a proficient writer. Immediately, Kim put the set to use. He ground some of the ink in water and dipped his brush into it. On a piece of paper he wrote *Ah Buh Ji*, which means "father."

In his letter, Kim Hyong Jik wrote about events in Manchuria and Russia. He explained that in Russia the workers, peasants, and other toiling people were in charge. He was envious of their lives. That night, the family read Kim Hyong Jik's letter again and again under the dim light of a kerosene lamp. After the rest of the family went to bed, Kim read the letter once more aloud to his mother.

Kim's father was jailed for several months for his involvement with a resistance group called the Korean People's Association. When Kim Hyong Jik was released from prison, he returned home to his family. His arrest had placed him on a Japanese police blacklist. The police commanded Kim Hyong Jik to stay home and work on his farm. Kim's father had devoted his life to fighting for Korean liberation. He did not want to give up and spend the rest of his life farming quietly. He also knew, though, that under the watchful eye of the Japanese police, he could be of little help to Korean nationalists in Mangyong-dae. He decided to move his family to Joong-gang on the northern border of Korea.

The move was difficult for eight-year-old Kim. He did not want to leave the mountains and rivers of his childhood home. At the same time, Kim was happy to move far away from Pyongyang and the Japanese police who could throw his father back in prison at anytime. Kim believed that moving to a remote village, 250 miles (400 kilometers) from Mangyong-dae, would bring safety to his family.

Kim's family brought few possessions with them. Kang Bang Suk carried a bag containing her rice-cooking pot and a few spoons, and Kim's father carried a sack of clothing. These were all the belongings they took. They rode a train to Sinahnju (near Anju) and from there, the family walked most of the way to Joong-gang.

Kim's parents worried that Kim, being only eight years old, might not be able to make the long, hard trip, which passed through rugged terrain. Kim sometimes hitched rides on passing oxcarts, but he walked most of the way on his own feet. He later remembered, "It was the first major physical endurance test in my life." Crossing Mount

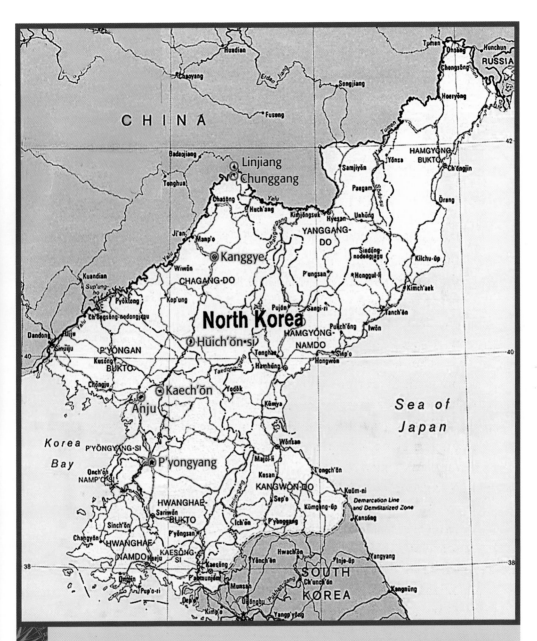

A map showing the travels of Kim Il Sung and his family as they left Mangyong-dae, near Pyongyang, for Joong-gang (Chunggang on this map) in 1920. Forced to flee after Kim's father had been placed on a blacklist by the Japanese police, the family took a train to Sinahnju (near Anju) and then traveled on foot to Joong-gang.

Bainang was a struggle for Kim's mother. Kim's brother, Chul Ju, was only three years old. Kang Bang Suk carried Chul Ju in her arms and a bundle on her head. The soles of her shoes were worn through, and the long trip left bleeding blisters on her feet.

When they arrived in Joong-gang, Kim was disappointed by what he saw. The village was overrun with Japanese, not much different from Mangyong-dae and Pyongyang. More than half of Joong-gang was occupied by Japanese immigrants, who operated a Japanese school, a hospital, and numerous shops. Joong-gang had a Japanese police station, a military post, and a jail. Kim recalled, "Joong-gang made me realize that all of Korea was a gigantic dungeon."

Kim learned that the main reason his father had chosen to move to Joong-gang was because it was a hub of the Korean nationalist movement. Anti-Japanese leaflets circulated in the streets, and students boycotted classes. Kim Hyong Jik planned to open a hospital in Joong-gang. As a medical doctor, he thought he could escape the strict surveillance of the Japanese police. He also felt that being a doctor would allow him to see more people and be better informed about nationalist activities.

After a year in Joong-gang, the Japanese police suspected Kim Hyong Jik of anti-Japanese activities. Upon further investigation, they learned about Kim Hyong Jik's history in Pyongyang. He was once again placed on a blacklist. Soon afterward, Kim's father found out that he was going to be arrested. He decided the family must move at once. This time, they had to flee Korea to Manchuria, a part of China.

The news of the move deeply depressed Kim. Leaving Mangyong-dae had been difficult enough, but leaving Korea was unimaginable. Kim later wrote, "Man's life is full of sorrows and, of all the sorrows, the sorrow of losing one's country is the worst." Kim's family departed on a gloomy fall morning. Kim sadly watched flocks of migrating birds flying south in the sky above him. As his feet took their last steps on Korean soil, a brisk wind blew helpless fallen leaves in circles on the ground.

3

Two Hundred Fifty Miles to School

Moving to a foreign country filled Kim with fear. He could not imagine moving to a new land where he was unfamiliar with the language and where no one welcomed him. Kim's father tried to comfort him by telling him that tens of thousands of other Koreans had to flee their homes, too, leaving everything they owned behind.

When his family arrived in Lim-gang, China, everything looked strange to Kim. The town, a thriving commercial center, bustled with activity. All the people seemed to be in a hurry to do their business. One thing stood out as a bright spot amid Kim's fear and uncertainty. He saw only a few Japanese in Lim-gang. The Japanese had little influence in Manchuria at that time and had to use secretive methods to attack Korean nationalists living there. This made Lim-gang safer for Kim's family than Joong-gang had been.

A street in Manchuria in the 1920s. Kim Il Sung's family, again persecuted by the Japanese police, moved from Joong-gang in Korea to Lim-gang in Manchuria.

Soon after the family settled in Lim-gang, Kim's father hired a Chinese tutor to teach Kim, who also began attending Lim-gang Elementary School. Kim's tutor gave him extra lessons in the Chinese language. After much hard work,

Kim became fluent in Chinese. He later attended Paldo-gu Elementary School. Kim Hyong Jik also gave Kim lessons in Korean language, geography, and history as well as on Leninism and the ideology of Sun Yat-sen of China. Because Kim Hyong Jik felt education was very important, he was strict with Kim and his brother. If they did poorly in their studies, their father would punish them severely.

However, not all of Kim's childhood was shrouded with seriousness and studies. Like any other ten-year-old, Kim played games and had adventures with his friends. Once, Kim cut a hole about three feet (one meter) in diameter through the ice of the frozen Yalu River. Kim and his friends took turns jumping over the hole. As they jumped, Kim taunted the other children. He claimed that any child unable to jump the hole would never be accepted in the Korean army. None of the children wanted to be left out. Weak and strong alike lined up to take a leap over the hole. Some children were too young to make the jump and fell into the icy water. They quickly ran home—half frozen in their wet clothing. Parents often blamed Kim for coming up with dangerous stunts and leading the other children into them. Kim later recalled, "I was known as the Paldo-gu gang leader, and parents blamed me for the misdeeds of their kids."

Even as a young child, Kim was constantly surrounded by his father's passion for Korea. Kim learned that dedication to the nationalist movement and independence was a commitment required of all Koreans. From time to time, Kim's father asked him to run errands for Korean nationalists. Kim often carried secret messages from his father to other nationalists. On one occasion, Kim went back to Joong-gang to pick up a load of bullets and gunpowder. Kim hid the items in his schoolbag. He watched the customs inspectors comb through belongings and check the handbags and pockets of every adult passing into China. The Japanese police, however, were less inclined to check the belongings of children. They let

Kim pass without checking his bag, and he safely returned home as a successful runner for the Korean nationalists.

RETURNING HOME

Early in 1923, Kim Hyong Jik told Kim he would be continuing his studies in Korea. This news shocked Kim—moving from place to place with his family had been difficult enough, but traveling without them was unimaginable. Kim's father insisted that, as a native Korean, Kim should know his homeland and the suffering his people endured. Eleven-year-old Kim wondered if he had the courage to make the 250-mile (400-kilometer) journey alone, crossing steep mountains and uninhabited forests. At the same time, the thought of returning home to Mangyong-dae excited him.

Kim Hyong Jik drew a detailed map, including instructions for safe places to stop in Kanggye and Pyongyang. Meanwhile, Kim's mother packed a bag and sewed a new coat and cotton-padded socks for Kim to wear. Kim left Paldo-gu during a snowstorm on March 16, 1923. Some of his friends walked with him. They accompanied him all the way to Huchang after crossing the Yalu River. Kim's friends wanted to continue traveling with him, but Kim finally persuaded them to return home.

During his trip, Kim suffered many hardships. Crossing the mountains was difficult, and he was afraid of wild animals, even in daylight. It took Kim an entire day to cross Mount Ohga. "I walked and walked; there was no end in sight, and new mountains popped up in my way," he remembered. Throughout his trip, Kim was also taken aback by the kindness and generosity of the Korean people. Many Koreans took him into their homes or hotels, accepting little or no money for food, shelter, and a warm bed.

As the sun was setting on March 29, Kim reached the doorstep of his old home. His grandmother dropped her laundry and rushed to greet him. Through the night, Kim's relatives listened to stories about his family and asked many questions about his father and mother. The next morning, Kim once again laid eyes on the majestic rivers and mountainsides of his home village, their beauty unchanged. He also noticed, however, that more Koreans lived in poverty than ever before. After visiting his father's family, Kim moved in with his mother's family in Chilgol.

Several days after his arrival, Kim enrolled in the fifth grade at Changduk Elementary School, a private Korean school set up by his mother's father, Grandpa Kang, and other progressive residents of Chilgol. Kim noticed changes among the schoolchildren. Some students spoke Japanese, even in the classrooms. After school, children who could speak Japanese taught the language to other students. This disregard for Korean culture bothered Kim, who told the children trying to learn Japanese that they should speak Korean.

Many of Kim's Changduk schoolmates wanted to learn Chinese. Since they knew Kim had spent several years in Manchuria, they assumed he could speak fluent Chinese. They often asked him to speak Chinese to them. Kim refused, saying, "Why use Chinese when we have our own language?"

Even in school, Kim worked to build Korean patriotism. On one occasion, Kim and 12 other students put together a musical play called *Thirteen Collection*. Each child represented a province of Korea. In the production, the 13 children would hold up a cardboard map of their province, while dancing and singing Korean songs on stage. Near the end, the 13 children would arrange their cardboard provinces in the shape of Korea. Halfway through the play, the Japanese police burst into the room and stopped the show.

THE SKIES FELL

After two years of study, Kim's grandfather received horrifying news. Kim Hyong Jik had been arrested again. "The skies fell on me. I shook with anger and boiled with hatred for

Japan," Kim recalled. With only a few months until graduation, Kim decided to pack his bags and return to his mother in Paldo-gu.

Kim made it to the Yalu River in 14 days. The ten-foot-wide (three-meter-wide) river was frozen, and a handful of footsteps would carry him quickly across. He knew his mother and brothers were just beyond the other side, but something held him back. It pained him to leave Korea again. He bent down and picked up a pebble. Holding it tightly in his hand, he carried that small piece of Korea across the Yalu. As he walked on the frozen water, he said, "Korea, Korea, I must leave you now . . . but I shall forget you not. Korea wait for me—I shall return."

Kim reached home after dark. He opened the door and found his mother working calmly. Happy to see him, she threw her arms around him and gave him a firm hug. She told Kim she was very proud of him for making such a long and dangerous journey twice. Kim told her about their relatives back home. He then asked about his father. Kim's mother whispered softly that he was okay, but did not say any more. From her expression, Kim could see that his father was still in danger.

After dinner, Kim planned to unpack his bag and spend a quiet night playing with his brothers, but that was not to be. Kim's mother told him to take his brothers and leave at once. She told him the family was not safe, that Japanese spies were watching their every move. Some friends in Lim-gang would be waiting for the boys, and they would be safe there. Kang Bang Suk said she would wait for Kim's uncle and meet them there shortly. She said Kim must leave while it was still dark, when he could escape without being noticed. She had arranged a sleigh ride for the boys to Lim-gang.

Fourteen-year-old Kim was dumbfounded. After a 14-day walk and without a good night's rest, he was expected to make another journey—this time with his two younger brothers.

The Yalu River forms the border between North Korea and China. When Kim was returning to Manchuria after two years of schooling in Korea, he was pained to have to cross the river and leave his homeland.

The night was cold and windy. The dark forests that surrounded the road to Lim-gang reminded Kim of his long and lonely trip home. The three boys huddled under a heavy quilt, Kim's brothers clinging tightly to his arms. Kim was not sure what made him shiver more—the icy wind or the fear welling up inside him.

The next day, they arrived at the house of Roh Gyong Doo, a good friend of Kim's father. Kim's mother kept her word and soon joined them in Lim-gang. The family stayed with Roh for about a month, during which time he shared all that he owned. Kim later described his late-night run to Lim-gang: "I realized that revolution was no picnic."

4

Whasung Military Academy

Kim's father soon escaped from prison at Popyong with the help of a friend. During his escape, Kim Hyong Jik ran on foot over snow-covered paths, causing him to suffer severe frostbite. He eventually made it to the town of Musong. He immediately phoned his family in Lim-gang, asking them to join him.

When Kim arrived in Musong, he was overjoyed to see his father. He ran to Kim Hyong Jik with tears running down his cheeks. After a long embrace, Kim took a good look at his father. Kim Hyong Jik looked ill and weak; it was obvious that prison and the escape had taken a toll on him. Before long, Kim Hyong Jik's condition worsened, and he developed a severe cough that did not get better. On June 5, 1926, Kim's father died.

Kim was devastated by his father's death. Until then, he had looked to his father for guidance, advice, and answers. Now

Kim Il Sung in a military uniform. As a teenager, after his father's death, Kim attended Whasung Military School, which trained officers to fight for Korean independence. He found the training outdated.

14-year-old Kim was left to support his family. He vowed to follow in his father's footsteps and devote his life to fighting for Korea's independence.

Several weeks after Kim Hyong Jik's death, Kim enrolled in Whasung Military School in Whajun. The academy was a two-year school that trained army officers to fight for independence. The curriculum focused on military training and political education. Whasung also offered classes in Korean history, biology, geography, mathematics, and world revolution. Whasung mainly accepted soldiers with combat experience. Kim wondered whether he, with no military experience, would fit in with the rest of the students.

When Kim arrived at Whasung, he was surprised by the battered appearance of the school building and dormitory. He was expecting a bolder-looking structure. He tried to remind himself that the building's appearance was unimportant; what happened inside was what mattered. The school's director, Choe Dong Oh, greeted Kim. Choe knew Kim's father and was excited to have Kim at Whasung. "You are here at an opportune moment," he told Kim. "Our independence move is in a dire need of new talents. . . . Japanese use new tactics and weapons against us, and we need new tactics and weapons to counter them. Who can do this for us? Young people like you must come out with solutions for us."

Kim started school the next day. As he looked around the classroom, Kim saw students of all ages—some old enough to be his uncles. Choe introduced him to the class as Kim Hyong Jik's son, and the students clapped wildly. Kim was quickly accepted as a member of the Whasung student body.

Having had much more schooling than most of the other students, Kim found the courses rather simple and unchallenging. Most of the other students had quit school at a young age to fight the Japanese. Therefore, their study skills were somewhat rusty. Many found mathematics particularly difficult. One day, Kim stood at the blackboard and solved a difficult math problem with ease. The other students were thoroughly impressed. From that day forward, Kim helped them with their math lessons. In return, the men told Kim stories about fighting the Japanese. They also gave Kim tips on how to tackle tough military exercises.

Despite the fact that Kim took pride in training to become a nationalist fighter, he thought many of the Whasung trainers' combat tactics, political views, and military strategies were outdated. He later wrote, "Every time I was made to run with sand bags wrapped around my legs, I had to wonder, 'How on earth will this help me defeat the Japanese?'" He was also disappointed with the ideology held by many students and instructors on the type of government Korea should have after independence. Some students believed Korea should restore the old monarchy. Others insisted that capitalism was the only way to protect Korea from again being overrun by another nation.

During a class debate, Kim expressed his ideas for a new Korean government. He did not believe Korea should have a European-style government. To Kim, this type of government exploited the working class by allowing the rich to become richer off the work of the poor. He also pointed out that restoring the monarchy would be foolish, since the royal family was responsible for selling out Korea in the first place. Instead, Kim felt Korea should establish a society without class exploitation, a country in which all people were equal and where the working class was in control. After class, Choe approached Kim and shook his hand. "You did a good job of preaching Communism without mentioning 'Communism,'" he said.

IN JILIN

The longer that Kim stayed at Whasung Military Academy, the more eager he became to find a way to fight for Korea. He strongly believed that a new approach to gaining independence must be taken. He became frustrated with what he called the "outdated, feudalistic curriculum" of Whasung. Kim wondered if he should continue his studies there or find another school. Because he wanted to honor his family, he was reluctant to leave Whasung. But after much struggling, Kim decided to quit and attend a middle school in the city of Jilin.

Jilin was a political hot spot for Korean activists in Manchuria. Many Koreans called it the "Second Shanghai," because Shanghai was the center of Korean nationalist activity. Although Kim's mother was disappointed at first that he was quitting the academy, she supported his decision upon hearing his reasons. She told him, "Now that you have made up your mind, make sure you take giant steps."

Before leaving his mother in Musong, Kim formed the New Age Children's League, a group to promote patriotism among Korean children from the surrounding area. The Children's League supported the ideas of communism and departed from old political customs. Kim also helped his mother organize the Anti-Japan Women's Association. Through this organization, Kim's mother taught women and girls the Korean language and about the revolution. In early 1927, Kim left his family, bound for Jilin and filled with renewed hope and determination.

About this time, groups of Korean activists tried to unite and form an alliance. They eventually joined into three groups—Jungyi Command, Sinmin Command, and Chamyi Command. The three commands refused to cooperate with each other, and their factionalism made them easy prey for Japanese troops. Kim was disgusted by the disunity of the nationalists and Communists who were supposed to be fighting for the same goal—Korean independence. He believed that the key to victory was unity. He saw much strength in the younger generation. He also stood firmly behind the progressive ideologies of Marxism-Leninism, which was rapidly gaining popularity among the youth.

Kim decided to try to form an organization for Jilin's young people. Its mission would be to instill an anti-Japanese spirit, train young Koreans in progressive ideas, and encourage them to spread these ideas to others. Other groups already existed, but Kim wanted to develop his own association, in which he could play a leading role. In April 1927, Kim and other Korean activists officially established the Korean Jilin Teens' Association.

That summer, the group ran a language school, teaching Korean to Korean students attending Chinese schools. Many of these teens had lived in China their entire lives and knew Chinese better than Korean. The organization's slogan became "Koreans must know Korea."

During his school days in Jilin, Kim spent many hours attending the secret meetings of Korean nationalists. At these meetings he often gave lectures or orchestrated public debates. In time, association leaders saw a growing need to consolidate the numerous groups. The groups joined together to form the Young Korean Communist Association.

JILIN-DUNHUA RAILWAY PROJECT

In the summer of 1928, the Young Korean Communist Association held rallies to protest the Japanese imperialist troops who were planning to take over Manchuria. During several northward expeditions by the Japanese troops, many Chinese people were murdered. To create a link from Japanese-occupied Korea to Manchuria, the Japanese planned to build a railway between Jilin and the northern Korean border town of Hoeryong.

Chinese and Korean activists needed to organize a demonstration to warn the Japanese that the Chinese people would not tolerate an invasion of Manchuria. Because the Young Korean Communist Association was an underground organization, other groups decided that it should not participate in overt actions. Kim, however, was involved in planning a demonstration to be held in Jilin during an inauguration ceremony of the Jilin-Dunhua railway.

On the day of the demonstration, thousands of students, both Korean and Chinese, marched down the streets of Jilin screaming, "Down with Japanese imperialist aggressors! Stop the Jilin-Hoeryong [Jilin-Dunhua] line project!" During the rally, Kim called out to the demonstrators, asking Koreans and Chinese to unite against the Japanese. Intimidated by the demonstrations, the Japanese railway company postponed the inauguration. As the rally raged, windows of businesses were smashed, and many Japanese shopkeepers fled their stores. Incidents surrounding the building of the railway sparked armed struggles between the Japanese and Chinese.

As news about the rally spread throughout Manchuria and Korea, many Japanese learned about the youth and student movement in Jilin. The rally sent the Japanese police hot on the protesters' trail, planting spies throughout Manchuria. Before long, leaders of youth movements—including Kim—were captured and tortured in an attempt to uncover underground activities. Kim and other leaders refused to talk about their organizational network. In May 1929, Kim was sent to a prison in Jilin. He was placed in a northern cell, which received no warmth from sunlight during the day. In summer, the cell was musty and hot. In winter, frost covered the walls.

Kim refused to discontinue his work, even though he was in prison. He decided that, in order to keep in contact with Korean organizations, he needed a liaison to the outside world. The best way to achieve this was to win the sympathy of a warder. Much to his surprise, Kim quickly won the respect of one warder. The man agreed to deliver messages first to other cellmates and later to people on the outside.

THE NORTHEAST ANTI-JAPANESE UNITED ARMY

Late in 1929, Kim was released from prison. By this time, the situation in Manchuria had grown tense—armed soldiers and police officers walked the streets searching people and houses. Since Kim's capture, there had been many violent struggles. The Chinese people refer to this period of violence and unrest in Manchuria as the Red May Struggle.

Around this time, Kim Sung Ju changed his name to Kim Il Sung. The name *Il Sung* means "one star" and was given to Kim by his comrades. He also began engaging in partisan activities in southern Manchuria. He joined an army of Chinese guerrilla fighters against the Japanese. By 1932, the Chinese guerrilla factions joined together to form the Northeast Anti-Japanese United Army, of which 20-year-old Kim was a member. The Chinese commander Yang Jingyu led the group.

The United Army was divided into six smaller armies to fight on different fronts in Manchuria. The soldiers of these armies consisted of thousands of youth volunteers as well as members of the Chinese and Korean Communist parties and armed anti-Japanese nationalist groups. The total fighting force of the Chinese numbered about 15,000. Kim fought in the 2nd Army, formed in 1934, of the United Army.

Kim began his military career as a fighter in a small detachment of the 2nd Army. He made notable accomplishments and gained the respect of his commanders. Kim quickly rose in the ranks, eventually becoming 6th Division commander. In 1936, the 2nd and 5th armies joined in an operation against the Japanese. Kim was appointed political commissar (head of the army branch in charge of food and supplies) under the Chinese commander Chai Shiying. He also served as commander of his own division—the Kim Il Sung Division—numbering about 100 men. Kim's division was stationed in the Emu area, between Jilin and Manchuria. After the death of the 2nd Army commander, Wei Zhengmin took over and became Kim's mentor.

It was during his guerrilla days that Kim became truly well known among Chinese and Korean revolutionaries and the Japanese police. His largest and most successful campaign was a raid waged on the Korean town of Poch'ŏnbo, just beyond the Manchurian border. At the time, Kim was commanding a group of 200 guerrillas in the 6th Division of the 2nd Army. On June 4, 1937, Kim's army attacked, destroying local Japanese government offices and setting fire to the Japanese police station, elementary school, and post office. The 6th Division occupied Poch'ŏnbo for a day, then retreated to Manchuria. The Japanese police pursued Kim's troops and caught up with them at the Yalu River. Kim turned his army around and commanded the men to fight, defeating the Japanese police and killing seven officers. This raid brought Kim recognition among the Japanese and established him as a famous anti-Japanese fighter.

During 1938 and 1939, Kim continued to fight with the United army, mainly in southern and southeastern Manchuria. In 1939, the Japanese launched a number of expeditionary forces to control the Communist guerrillas in Manchuria. The Japanese army was particularly interested in securing bases in Manchuria to support its projected advance into other parts of China. In addition, the Japanese wanted to gain control of Chinese natural resources, including coal and timber. In October 1939, leaders of the Japanese military met with representatives of the Manchurian government to discuss how to stop the Chinese guerrilla fighters. They decided to implement a "submission operation," in which guerrilla leaders would be offered money and immunity in exchange for surrender. The operation was an immediate success. Those who surrendered not only vowed to abandon communism, but also assisted in capturing other guerrilla leaders.

As word of the Japanese expedition and the guerrilla surrenders spread, the United Army reorganized itself into three directional armies. The armies fought together under the 1st Route Army. In this reorganization, Kim served as commander of the 2nd Directional Army. The Japanese intensified their campaign, and eventually, all guerrilla leaders except Kim either surrendered or were killed. On January 30, 1941, the 1st Route Army was defeated with the surrender of political commissar Chŏn Kwang. Chŏn led Japanese troops directly to the hideouts of his comrades, ultimately dissolving the United Army.

Although Kim continued to fight until the end, it became apparent that the United army was defeated. Shortly after the death of Wei in March 1941, Kim fled to the Soviet Union for safety. Kim and six other men followed the banks of the Tumen

Japanese troops enter a town in Manchuria, China, during the Sino-Japanese War in the 1930s. In 1939, the Japanese sent a number of forces to try to control Communist guerrillas in Manchuria.

River to the west of Vladivostok. Once in the Soviet Union, Kim joined a Chinese guerrilla group with three training camps led by Zhou Baozhong, a United Army commander who had fled China in 1940. The training camps operated in three locations: Okeanskaya Field School near Vladivostok, Voroshilov Camp in Nikolsk, and a wooded area to the south of Khabarovsk. There, Kim would learn the skills he needed to fight for the freedom of his nation.

5

Liberation!

During Kim's nearly five-year stay in the Soviet Union, he married a female soldier named Kim Chǒng-suk (in Kim's memoirs, her name is spelled "Kim Jong Suk"). Twenty-two-year-old Kim Jong Suk had fought in Kim's guerrilla army in Manchuria. She cooked, sewed, and washed the guerrillas' clothes, often sacrificing her own comfort for that of her comrades. On one occasion, she and several other women soldiers fired heavily at Japanese soldiers to save Kim's life. Another time, Kim Jong Suk ran through gunfire and delivered hot dumplings to the soldiers while they fought. She once cut her hair to make warm pads for the bottom of Kim's shoes.

Kim and Kim Jong Suk did not have a formal wedding or any celebration. Their wedding was simple: They just announced their marriage and then went on with their usual activities within the

Kim Il Sung, his wife, Kim Jong Suk, and their son Kim Jong Il, in a family portrait taken around 1946. Kim Jong Il was born on February 16, 1942, after his parents had fled to the Soviet Union.

platoon. Kim later wrote about guerrilla weddings, "Some couples went into battle immediately after their weddings and fell in action, and other couples lived apart, as they were given different missions." Throughout their marriage, Kim Jong Suk did not address Kim in casual terms. She always referred to him as "General" or "Comrade Premier."

On February 16, 1942, Kim Jong Suk gave birth to a son, Kim Jong Il. While still in the Soviet Union in 1944, Kim Jong Suk had another son, Kim P'yŏng-il—who was often called "Shura."

By 1943, Soviet troops were engaged in a full-scale war with Germany on their eastern front in World War II. At the same time, the United States was at war with Japan and Germany. When German forces surrendered in May 1945, Kim and his men celebrated with their Soviet comrades as if it were their own victory. It seemed inevitable to Kim that Japan would be the next to fall. Kim remembered, "The fascist forces that had once been rampant in the world were now tumbling one after the other to the grave in both the East and the West. Now it was Japan's turn to take the baton."

During the summer of 1945, the Soviet Union began planning an invasion of Manchuria. After air bombing, the Soviet forces planned to attack the fortified areas along the coast. Infantry units would push through Manchuria with armored vehicles. The Chinese and Korean Communist armies dispatched many small groups and guerrilla units to Korea and Manchuria. They also assigned the people's armed corps and resistance organizations to destroy all remnants of Japanese colonial rule and protect the lives and property of Koreans.

On August 6, 1945, an American bomber plane dropped the first atomic bomb on Hiroshima, Japan, killing thousands instantly and flattening buildings within a 1.5-mile (2.4-kilometer) radius. The world had not yet seen such explosive power in action. Two days later, the Soviet Union declared war on Japan, and Soviet troops invaded Manchuria. Kim's army also participated in this attack. Their battles did not last long, however. On August 9, the United States dropped a second atomic bomb, this time on Nagasaki. Five days later, Japan made an unconditional surrender. Korea was finally free from Japanese rule.

THE LIBERATORS

Koreans greeted their American and Soviet liberators with intense jubilation. As a country, Korea did not necessarily approve of either American or Soviet ideologies, but at least Japanese rule had come to an end. Almost immediately, party organizations and people's committees formed, headed by revolutionaries and resistance members. Literary people and artists gathered in Pyongyang, Seoul, and other major cities, eager to rebuild Korean culture. Koreans established armed guard units to protect factories, coal mines, ports, and railways from traitors and remnants of the Japanese army. The country split into two sections, divided along the 38th parallel of latitude, each occupied by a liberating army. American troops secured the southern part of Korea while the Soviet Union occupied the north.

In South Korea, the United States appointed 70-year-old Syngman Rhee as leader. Rhee had degrees from George Washington University, Harvard, and Princeton. Throughout most of the Japanese occupation, Rhee had lived in exile.

In the North, Kim faithfully carried out Soviet commands, placing himself in a leadership role. Kim helped create a new army, a new political party, and a new government, all of which were modeled after the Soviet Communist system. Ultimately, the Soviet Union chose Kim to be the leader of liberated North Korea. Although Kim had made many accomplishments as a guerrilla fighter, he was not a national hero. Still, Kim was a Korean Communist whom the Soviet Union had trained, who freely wore the Soviet uniform in battle, and whose record as an anti-Japanese guerrilla fighter was well known. Kim had little opposition to his leadership position. Most prominent Korean political leaders were in the South, negotiating with the Americans.

After 20 years spent in foreign lands, Kim returned home to Pyongyang on September 22, 1945. He immediately got busy carrying out the tasks of building the state, the army, and the political party. He visited factories and rural communities, and he attended many meetings with political leaders and advisors.

On October 14, Kim was scheduled to meet the people for the first time. About noon, he went to the Pyongyang public playground, where a platform had been erected for him. Thousands of people crowded the park and filled the surrounding streets. As Kim stepped onto the platform, the crowds shouted, "Long live the independence of Korea!" Kim was overcome with emotion at the happy cries of the people. "If anyone asked me about the happiest moment in my life, I would reply that it was that moment," Kim wrote. "It was happiness emanating from the pride that I had fought for the people as a son of the people, from the feeling that the people loved and trusted me, and from the fact that I was in the embrace of the people."

After Kim spoke, he returned to his village home in Mangyong-dae. The yard looked much smaller to him that day than it had 20 years earlier. Kim's mother had died in 1932 while Kim was fighting with the guerrilla army, but his grandparents were still living. They asked Kim many questions about his wife and sons, who had not yet returned to Pyongyang. That night, Kim slept in his family home for the first time since he was a boy.

PROCLAIMING HIS REPUBLIC

In October 1945, the North Korean Communist Party was established, with Kim the appointed leader of the Soviet occupation authorities. This party later joined with the New Democratic Party to become the Workers' Party of Korea. At first, Kim did not serve as chairman of the party. Kim Tu-bong, who had been chairman of the New Democratic Party, was elected chairman. Kim Il Sung served as vice chairman. However, the Soviet occupation authorities gave their full support to Kim Il Sung as leader, and by 1948, Kim took over as chairman of the party as well.

From 1945 to 1948, the United States and the Soviet Union tried to work out an agreement for dividing Korea. Kim was opposed to the idea of two separate governments in Korea. To prove this point, he waited until South Korea established its own government before he announced a republic in the North. In August 1948, the Republic of Korea was established in the South. Less than a month later, a Communist republic was created in the North. On September 10, 1948, Kim was elected the first premier of the Democratic People's Republic of Korea.

With the republic established, Kim went to work building a strong military army to sustain it. This was an important step in the development of an independent country. Within the first year, about 40,000 men were enlisted in the newly established Korean People's Army, many of whom were sent to Manchuria and the Soviet Union for training.

THE KOREAN WAR

Near the end of 1948, the Soviet Army completely withdrew from North Korea, leaving it under the authority of the government it had created. In June 1949, U.S. troops also left South Korea. Since liberation, Kim had a burning desire to reunite his entire homeland. He believed that the only way to achieve the reunification of Korea was by force. On several occasions in 1949 and 1950, Kim requested the support of Soviet leader Joseph Stalin and his Soviet diplomats in an invasion of South Korea. At one point, he told officers of the Soviet Embassy, "Lately I do not sleep at night, thinking about how to resolve the question of the unification of the whole country."

In the spring of 1950, Kim was awarded the support he wanted. On June 25, North Korean troops, backed by China and the Soviet Union, invaded South Korea. The result was the Korean War, which had a substantial effect on world politics. The war began a bitter 20-year relationship between China and

U.S. 1st Cavalry Division infantrymen, supported by tanks from the 24th Division, assault an enemy-held hill in South Korea in February 1951. About 520,000 North Korean soldiers were killed or wounded in the Korean War, which lasted from 1950 to 1953.

the United States and secured an alliance between China and the Soviet Union. The war for Korea also marked the first major military confrontation of the Cold War, which would be the focus of world conflict for the next 40 years.

When the fighting ended in July 1953, the front line had only slightly tilted across the 38th parallel, where the battling had begun three years before. The losses were devastating—an estimated 900,000 Chinese and 520,000 North Korean soldiers were wounded or killed, along with 400,000 United Nations

Command troops, two-thirds of whom were South Koreans. More importantly, the Korean War created cold shoulders between the North and South, as family members fought against each other and people on each side suffered terrible losses at the hands of the other. In addition, Koreans lived with the fear that another war might break out at any time.

6

After the War

Meanwhile, Kim worked to rebuild the North right after the war. Three years of constant American bombing had taken its toll on North Korea's cities and countryside. Over the years, Kim had recovered from setbacks with even stronger resolve. His first priority was to restore heavy industry, such as armaments, coal mining, and timber. At the same time, he planned to develop agriculture and light industry. To do so, he would need financial backing. He met with the new Soviet leaders—after the death of Stalin in 1953—to ensure economic aid from them. Kim received a loan of one billion rubles—about $32 million—to rebuild destroyed industrial buildings and factories. Next, Kim traveled to Beijing, China, with an eight-member delegation. China was even more generous, lending North Korea 3 trillion Chinese yuan (more than $300 million) to be paid in two installments. In addition to

Kim Il Sung in 1950. After the Korean War, Kim developed a three-year economic plan that nationalized all industries. He placed an emphasis on heavy industry, cutting back on the production of consumer goods.

these loans, Kim spent six months traveling to Eastern European countries to collect relief aid.

Kim developed a three-year economic plan in which he nationalized all industries—bringing them under the government's complete control. In agriculture, Kim implemented experimental cooperatives, with the goal of transforming all farmland into cooperatives. This process was carried out in three stages. In the first stage, work teams performed only the labor collectively. The second stage introduced collectivization of land and labor, and distribution was calculated by the amount of work performed and the size of the farmland collectivized. By the third stage, complete socialist cooperatives existed, in which both the land and production were collectivized. The shares were then distributed in accordance with the amount of work performed.

Kim's plan met fierce opposition, both in the agrarian sector and from industry. The industries were not opposed to nationalization but rather to the emphasis on heavy industry. This approach sacrificed the basic needs of the people by cutting back on consumer goods. It also required a great deal of hard work in large industries. Many upper-class farmers strongly disapproved of the cooperatives, as they lost the ownership and profit of their lands. Kim believed his plan would exceed its production goals. By the end of his economic plan in 1956, however, North Korea had only taken a sliver of a step toward restoring the economy to its prewar status.

CHALLENGE OF THE YANAN GROUP

Although Kim received the support of Soviet authorities, winning the approval of the Korean political parties under him was a different story. During the occupation, Kim had been rivaled by three major groups. The largest was made up of Korean Communists—called the "domestic group." The second group consisted of revolutionaries who lived in China until after Korean independence. They called themselves the New Democratic Party, more commonly referred to as the "Yanan group." The third of Kim's rivals was made up of Soviet-Koreans who marched into Korea with the Soviet Army but remained after Soviet occupational authorities withdrew. These three groups were never an overwhelming threat to Kim, because they were not united in supporting a single political leader. Their disunity kept them from gaining power.

From June 1 to July 19, 1956, Kim led a ten-member delegation to visit nine countries in Eastern Europe to solicit funds for his new five-year economic plan. Among the countries visited were East Germany, Poland, Romania, and the Soviet Union. This tour was less successful than Kim's first, primarily because three years had passed since the Korean War and the devastation Koreans faced was no longer fresh in the minds of the Eastern Europeans. This time around, the Soviet Union was Kim's biggest benefactor.

While Kim was abroad, Pak Ch'ang-ok of the Soviet faction and Yanan group leader Ch'oe Ch'ang-ik conspired to over-throw him. They wanted to replace his authoritarian rule with a collective leadership. Ch'oe claimed that it was time for a new government—abandoning communism in favor of a neutral Korea. He based his claims on the difficulties in economic recovery and on how the emphasis on heavy industry had placed undue hardship on the workers. Kim cut his trip short and returned home to deal with the conspirators.

Kim spent more than a year eliminating all antiparty participants before he returned to affairs of the state. In an attempt to control challenging members, Kim issued a new party identification card. From late 1956 to early 1957, Kim examined each member to evaluate his or her stance or participation in the conspiracy. Many members of Kim's government were prosecuted; most were expelled from the party and barred from all government activities.

THE SINO-SOVIET DISPUTE

During the 1960s, Kim found himself facing a growing clash between China and the Soviet Union. Soviet leaders had begun a process of de-Stalinization, in which the government began eliminating the political policies, methods, and personal image of the former leader Joseph Stalin—on which the Soviet

Union had been built. The Chinese strongly disapproved of these changes. Kim was stuck in the middle of the dispute, which led to separate conflicts between North Korea and the Soviet Union and North Korea and China.

After founding the People's Republic of China in 1949, Chinese leaders turned their focus to national security, consolidation of power, and economic development. Their goal was to form a united front with the Soviet Union and other socialist nations against the United States and Japan. Chinese Premier Mao Zedong negotiated the 1950 Sino-Soviet Treaty of Friendship, Alliance, and Mutual Assistance. Under the agreement, China allowed the Soviet Union continued use of a naval base at Luda (in Liaoning Province) in exchange for military support, weapons, economic assistance, and shared technological research. China recognized the Soviet Union as the leader of the Communist movement and as a model for developing countries to follow. China's participation in the Korean War strengthened relations with the Soviet Union.

By the late 1950s, though, Sino-Soviet relations had become strained over issues of ideology, security, and economics. After the death of Stalin, the Communist Party leader Nikita Khrushchev moved toward de-Stalinization. He also favored peaceful relations with the West. In 1957, the Soviets successfully launched the first Earth-orbiting satellite—*Sputnik*—convincing Mao that world dominance was tilted in the Communist direction. In response, Mao called for a stronger military policy against non-Communist countries. The Soviet Union, on the other hand, continued its stance in favor of peaceful relations.

In addition to ideological disagreements, Chinese leaders were unhappy with the Sino-Soviet security relationship. In the first place, the Soviets proposed a joint naval agreement in 1958 that put China in a militarily subordinate position. In 1959, the Soviet Union remained neutral during a border dispute between China and India. Soviet leaders were also reluctant to supply China with nuclear weapons technology. All of these issues violated the 1950 Sino-Soviet treaty. Ultimately, both China and the Soviet Union wanted to exercise independence and self-reliance more than they wanted to form a strong alliance.

The Sino-Soviet dispute put Kim in a precarious position. He wanted to avoid taking sides against either of his two greatest benefactors. Instead, Kim called for unity and cooperation among all socialist countries, praising both the Soviet Union and China on different counts. He pointed out that the Soviet Union had been the wall of protection for the revolutionary movement for 40 years. Thus, it was the duty of all socialist countries to support it. On the Sino-Indian border conflict, the North Korean government expressed its support for China against India, but did not directly attack the Soviets for their lack of involvement. Despite trying to remain neutral, North Korea came out appearing to have a pro-China and anti-Soviet stance in the end. Kim had been a strong supporter and a great admirer of Stalin's. For this reason, he did not agree with Khrushchev's political or economic policies and views.

After Khrushchev was forced from power in 1964, Kim tried to restore relations with the Soviet Union. This effort angered the Chinese, especially a radical militant group of Mao supporters called the Red Guard. The Red Guard began putting up posters all over China, condemning Kim's leadership and spreading rumors about Kim and his deputies.

More significant than the insults to Kim's government was a territorial dispute. The area in question involved Paektusan Mountain, which was sacred to North Koreans. The North Korea–China border is delineated by the Yalu and Tumen rivers. In between the two rivers stands Paektusan—the tallest mountain in Korea and northeastern China. The territory in dispute was an area that included 20 miles (32 kilometers) of the mountain and a volcanic lake at the

Kim Il Sung (right) with Chinese troops in 1958. In the late 1950s and early 1960s, Kim and North Korea were caught in the middle of the strained relationship between China and the Soviet Union.

top. Neither the Koreans nor the Chinese had explored the region to find its economic value, but both countries viewed the area as symbolic to them. Chinese legends claim that the Qing Dynasty originated from the mountain. Similarly, Korean mythology claims the Paektusan as the origin of the Korean kingdom. More important to Kim was the fact that he and his guerrilla fighters had conducted much of their revolutionary activities near the mountain. In fact, a song dedicated to Kim, "The Ballad of Kim Il Sung," begins with a reference to the mountain. Although the dispute did not lead to war, no agreement was ever reached.

During the Sino-Soviet dispute, Kim began to express North Korea's identity as an independent country. He said that each nation must "creatively apply Marxism and Leninism in accordance with its own national characteristics." Kim acknowledged the importance of the Soviet model, but also preached independence as self-reliance. He later wrote,

> [L]eaders of the Eastern European countries believed in the Soviet Union more than in the strength of their own people. Most of these countries were liberated by the Soviet Army, so they built socialism after the Soviet fashion, relying utterly on that country, and aping everything the Soviet people did and said. Their worship of the Soviet Union was so extreme that it was said that when it was raining in Moscow, they also raised their umbrellas. One of the reasons why socialism went to ruin in Eastern Europe was precisely the worship of the great power.

During the Sino-Soviet dispute, Kim firmly declared that North Korea would take no sides except that of Marxism and Leninism. In a speech to party members in October 1966, Kim said that Koreans would never "dance to the tune of others." He added that Korean Communists believed in cooperation between socialist countries, but based on equality and independence. With this speech, Kim formally declared North Korea independent of China and the Soviet Union.

7

Kim's Independence

After Kim declared his independence from China and the Soviet Union, he began vigorously building his army. Kim's emphasis on strengthening the military was partially linked to a fear of isolation. Once normal relations were restored with the Soviets, however, Kim used his swelling military strength for independent pursuits. To start, Kim began to form alliances with Third World countries, in an effort to isolate American imperialism.

Meanwhile, in South Korea, Rhee's government was becoming increasingly corrupt. A student revolt in 1960 forced his regime out of power. Major General Park Chung Hee later took over. Park was a Japanese-trained officer who had supported communism after World War II. With Park in office, Kim had renewed hope of reunification. He quickly sent a trusted emissary to the South for a secret meeting with Park, but Park refused to discuss a deal with the aide and had him executed.

The government in the South was in the course of building its political power by reaching normal relations with Japan—the first attempt since the end of Japanese colonial rule. In addition to strengthening these ties, South Korea was preparing to send troops to fight in the Vietnam War on the American side. This would be the first time in Korean history that troops were sent outside the country to fight.

Even after the Korean War, Kim had never given up his goal of reunifying Korea. He was waiting for the opportune time to incite a revolution in the South. Because the United Nations intervened on behalf of South Korea in the Korean War, there was virtually no resistance there to sending troops to South Vietnam. However, strengthening ties with Japan met with strong opposition. Kim felt that he could use this resistance to start a revolution.

UNIFICATION POLICY

In February 1964, Kim gave a lengthy speech on the unification of Korea. He believed successful reunification could take place through three revolutionary forces—one each in the North, in the South, and in the international sector. In North Korea, Kim again emphasized increasing its political, economic, and military capabilities. In the South Korean revolutionary force, Kim called for a unification of all small revolutionary organizations. South Koreans who had defected to the North were to be trained and returned to the South to participate in a revolution. To strengthen international forces, Kim used his close ties with Third World countries to push anti-imperialist sentiments. Kim ultimately hoped to form an international army of socialist and Communist countries to fight in Vietnam. With the Sino-Soviet dispute, though, such cooperation was impossible.

Nevertheless, Kim began to implement his unification

Kim Il Sung addressing a rally on North Korea's Liberation Day in 1966. In the late 1960s, Kim hoped to achieve the reunification of Korea by trying to incite a revolution in South Korea.

policy to try to foment a South Korean revolution in late 1967. The partisan generals dispatched a small guerrilla unit to the South that planned to assassinate South Korean President Park Chung Hee. The squad of 31 armed fighters crossed the 38th parallel near Kaesŏng on January 18, 1968. On the first night, the guerrillas camped near Pŏbwŏlli. They were immediately spotted by a couple of villagers, whom the guerrillas captured and released, warning them not to notify South Korean authorities. The villagers ignored the order. When the commando squad reached Seoul on January 21, it was met by the South Korean police. Twenty-seven of the guerrillas died in the skirmish, three others escaped, and one fighter was captured.

The prisoner was Kim Sin-jo. He revealed the assassination plans and told the South Korean police that many other guerrilla groups had been trained to infiltrate the South. A number of commando raids took place during 1968, all of which the South Korean police quickly stomped out. Meanwhile, Kim continued to urge South Koreans to revolt against their leaders. Kim, however, did not consider the fact that most South Koreans who opposed the treaty with Japan were also anti-Communist. For this reason, Kim's supposed uprisings caused minimal unrest in the South.

One of North Korea's biggest mistakes of the South Korean revolution was the capture of the American spy ship U.S.S. *Pueblo*. The ship was taken by surprise on January 23, 1968, and quickly surrendered. Although the easy seizure of an American vessel inflated the pride of the North Koreans, Kim was in no position to have a direct confrontation with the United States, especially given his strained relationships with China and the Soviet Union. North Korea escaped attack from the United States and released the American prisoners 11 months later, but Kim never returned the U.S.S. *Pueblo*.

Though armed guerrilla forces were intended to create short-term upset in South Korea, a more important attempt was made to implant a revolutionary party. One such group was known as the Revolutionary Party for Reunification (RPR). A South Korean Communist, Kim Chong-t'ae, founded the organization. Chong-t'ae formed nine other revolutionary organizations before his arrest in July 1968. With his arrest, the South Korean authorities were able to disband the RPR's operation, arresting 158 people involved with the party. Chong-t'ae was prosecuted and sentenced to death. His execution on January 24, 1969, marked the end of Kim's plan to create a revolutionary uprising in South Korea.

ATTEMPT AT "TALKS"

In early 1972, political realignments took place in East Asia. In late February, Chinese leaders met with U.S. President Richard M. Nixon. The talks led to a normalization of relations between China and the United States—a small step toward relieving tensions between the two countries. The Soviet foreign minister then arranged a Soviet-Japanese peace treaty. Also at this time, the Japanese prime minister signed a Sino-Japanese peace treaty in Beijing. Kim had learned his lesson from the Sino-Soviet dispute and refrained from commenting on the new relationships developing among the Soviet Union, China, and the United States. However, Kim verbally attacked the United States and interpreted the treaties as a sign of U.S. weakness, calling Nixon's visits "a great surrender of a defeated America."

Ch'oe Tusŏn, the South Korean Red Cross president, requested talks with North Korea in an effort to establish a program to reunite families separated in the North and South. The North Koreans agreed to meet with the representatives. Before any issues were discussed, Kim took credit for the talks, claiming that South Korea was forced to meet because the people of the South were "crying out" for relations with the North. The meeting ended with Kim agreeing to work on a program to reunite families.

More importantly, after the talks Kim agreed to discuss the issue of reunification through political conferences, rather than military force. After several meetings, on November 4, 1972, representatives from both sides established the North-South Coordinating Committee. The committee held three meetings over the next seven months. The first meeting took place from November 30 to December 2 in Seoul, South Korea. The second meeting was held in March in Pyongyang. Three months later, representatives again gathered in Seoul. But the third meeting was the committee's last—a fourth was scheduled but North Korea declined to attend.

The South Koreans wanted North Korea to recognize the separate political systems of the North and South. This recognition would include an agreement of noninterference in the international relations of either side. In addition, South Korea agreed to cooperate on a limited level in economic and sociocultural areas.

North Korea's position was very different. Kim wanted an independent nation without international interference, meaning the withdrawal of U.S. troops in South Korea. Kim stated, "Frankly speaking, to reunify the country independently means to force the United States imperialists out of South Korea." Kim also insisted that South Korea reduce its armed forces and put an end to military modernization. A third demand called for a revocation of the anti-Communist law and allowed for Northern revolutionary groups to reorganize in the South.

Because Kim refused to budge on these terms, South Korean President Park proposed that North and South Korea be entered into the United Nations as separate countries. This decision infuriated Kim, who saw the United Nations as a tool of American imperialism. After the talks ended in a standstill, Kim returned to his old methods of trying to overthrow southern leaders from within.

In August 1974, guerrilla fighters again tried to assassinate President Park. On August 15, a group of South Korean citizens and foreign diplomats gathered at the National Theater in Seoul to hear Park speak. The speech was part of the twenty-ninth anniversary celebration of South Korea's liberation from Japan. While Park was speaking, a loud popping sound came from the back of the theater. A man in a dark suit raced down the center aisle, firing his gun as he ran. Presidential security guards, their guns drawn, bolted on stage and returned fire. People in the crowd panicked, some dropping to the floor, others running out of the hall. In the middle of the commotion, South Korea's first lady fell limp from her chair. She died several hours later from a bullet wound to her head. A high-school girl, who was a member of the chorus singing for the national holiday, was also killed in the crossfire.

About this time, the North Koreans made preparations to infiltrate the South. They dug a complex system of tunnels in the demilitarized zone between North and South Korea. Twelve-person teams worked in shifts around-the-clock, supervised by engineers, technicians, and guards. Workers dug tunnels about four feet wide and three feet high (1.2 meters wide and one meter high). They reinforced the interior walls with concrete and equipped them with electric wiring, lighting, and compartments for storing weapons. The tunnels even had sleeping areas and a small railroad track for hauling out carts of dirt.

Three months after the attempted assassination, a South Korean Army squad on patrol investigated a strange cloud of steam rising from the high grass in the demilitarized zone. One soldier pushed his bayonet into the ground, which collapsed into a tunnel. As the soldiers began investigating the tunnel, a nearby North Korean guard post opened fire on them. This was the first military confrontation between the two sides in 20 months.

The North Koreans had failed in two attempts to assassinate Park. It was Park's central intelligence director who finally finished the job. On October 26, 1979, Park met for dinner with several Korean officials, including Kim Jae Kyu—director of the Korean Central Intelligence Agency. During the dinner, Park criticized director Kim for failing to stay informed on domestic disorders. One of Park's officials also scolded the director for not dealing with the political unrest properly. Director Kim pulled out a pistol and fatally shot the two men at point-blank range.

Although Kim approved of Park's assassination, he had not been involved in it. Two days later, Kim addressed the people on the situation in the South, condemning Western influences and praising the Communist North. "Our people are

South Korean Army soldiers patrol one of two tunnels that North Korea dug under the demilitarized zone in an attempt to infiltrate the South. The tunnels were equipped with electric wiring, lighting, and compartments to store weapons.

enjoying a happy life to the full," he said, "without any worries about food, clothing, medical treatment or education. . . . Our country is truly a socialist paradise." Kim hoped that Park's assassination would lead to a revolution. Much to his disappointment, it did not. In 1980, Chun Doo Hwan took over as president of South Korea.

In January 1979, China and the United States signed a Sino-American normalization treaty. The treaty forced North and South Korea to meet again to discuss unification. Nothing new was accomplished. Afterward, Kim announced that the North-South Coordinating Committee no longer existed in North Korea. Instead, he continued to undermine the government of the South by calling for meetings of revolutionary organizations.

A NEW CONSTITUTION

The North Koreans adopted a new constitution in December 1972. The constitution proclaimed North Korea as an independent state—free from the Communist powers that had created it and manipulated it in the past. A number of changes distinguished the new constitution from the old one. In it, the voting age was lowered from 18 to 17, and the capital was moved from Seoul to Pyongyang. The biggest change, however, was in the accepted Communist ideologies. Kim substituted his own political thoughts on communism, which he referred to as the *chuch'e* idea.

By definition, the *chuch'e* idea is the creative application of Marxism and Leninism to the conditions and circumstances of a particular country. Under this idea, Kim said that North Koreans should respect the experiences of other socialist countries. The Koreans should only adopt policies that benefit their country, though. As part of this principle, Kim encouraged self-reliance. To Kim, self-reliance was the key to independence, economic survival, and military defense. Kim claimed that *chuch'e* was the Korean revolution.

Kim's revolutionary tradition became the tradition of North Korea. In addition to these changes, the office of president was introduced, and, of course, Kim assumed that role. As president, Kim inherited numerous powers. He served as the head of state and as commander of the armed forces. Kim also became the chairman of the National Defense Committee. In essence, Kim was the supreme authority in North Korea, having the power to create and abolish treaties, grant pardons, and issue edicts. At this time, Kim also was awarded the Order of Double Hero, the highest honor in the country. The award was part of his sixtieth birthday celebration on April 15, 1972.

8

The
New Era

Kim made an important announcement in February 1977. He named his son—Kim Jong Il—his sole successor as leader of Korea. In a formal document, Kim directed members of the party to pledge their support to "the dear leader Kim Jong Il," and carry on the revolutionary torch from one generation to the next.

In April 1982, Kim was elected to serve as president for yet another four years. The election took place just before his seventieth birthday on April 15. For his birthday, the people held a huge celebration at which several monuments dedicated to Kim were unveiled. One was the North Korean Arch of Triumph—the world's tallest stone monument. Also dedicated was the Tower of Chuch'e and the Kim Il Sung stadium in Pyongyang. To show his loyalty to his father, Kim Jong Il oversaw the construction of the monuments.

Kim Jong Il, center, and Kim Il Sung, right, visit a construction site in Pyongyang. The elder Kim was called "Great Leader;" his son is now referred to as "Dear Leader."

SEMI-RETIREMENT

By the late 1980s, Kim had turned over most state and party affairs to his son. Even so, he continued to be seen by the party and the people as North Korea's leader. Kim also continued to make all final decisions on international issues. Although his authority was not challenged, Kim had lost much of his prestigious flair for the office. Much of this was due to the recent loss of many of his partisan friends, who were also aging. One of the greatest of these losses was Kim's longtime vice president and guerrilla comrade, Ch'oe Yong-gŏn. Several days before Kim's birthday, another of Kim's dear friends, Ch'oe Hyŏn, died. Ch'oe Hyŏn had fought with Kim in Manchuria and in the Korean War. He had also served under Kim on the Military Affairs Commission. Of all of Kim's partisans, Ch'oe Hyŏn was the only person who could speak to him privately at any time.

After his birthday, Kim made fewer guidance tours to the countryside, a task he had enjoyed in the past. Kim's son began to take over the tours and also assumed other responsibilities for his father. Kim seldom made public appearances and gave fewer speeches and interviews.

In his later years, Kim focused more on restoring relationships with former allies. In 1982, he traveled to Beijing and told the welcoming crowd, "Korea and China have an exceptional friendship. The relationship between the two countries is as inseparable as the lips and teeth in the true sense of the word." Later in 1984, Kim visited the Soviet Union and Eastern European countries. During a speech in the Soviet Union, Kim expressed his desire to restore friendly relations between the two countries.

After returning home from his trip, Kim began to present himself in a more relaxed manner. He began wearing a suit jacket and tie instead of the people's jacket he had worn since the birth of the republic in 1948. Kim's new appearance had an effect on the people as well. After years of drab workers' uniforms, people began to wear more colorful clothing.

RANGOON TERRORIST BOMBING

Kim hoped to achieve the unification of Korea during his lifetime, but he was unable to do so. He believed that his work would be carried on by his son. However, he continued to put distance between the North and South with terrorist activities. In October 1983, the North Koreans planned an assassination attempt on Chun Doo Hwan, the South Korean president. The assassination was to occur outside the Martyrs Mausoleum at the National Cemetery in Rangoon, Burma. Chun would be attending a wreath-laying ceremony in honor of Burma's founder. On October 9, a North Korean Army major awaited Chun's arrival at the mausoleum. Chun was late, and the Korean ambassador arrived before him. The army major mistook the ambassador for Chun and detonated a bomb. The powerful explosion killed four members of the South Korean cabinet, the ambassador to Burma, and 12 other officials. The Burmese police quickly arrested the North Korea military officers responsible for the attack. Before the attack, North Korea and Burma had had a close relationship. Afterward, Burma broke all diplomatic relations with North Korea.

After the Rangoon terrorist bombing, North Korea began to change its reunification policy. The first noticeable sign came in September 1984 when the North Korean Red Cross Society offered to send relief items to flood victims in the South. It sent about 7,000 tons of rice, medical supplies, cement, and clothing. This relief was the first goodwill offer made and accepted by both sides. In November 1984, the North and South met to discuss economic proposals. Unlike what had happened in past meetings, the South was allowed an equal voice in the proposals. The most important sign of change was a delegation of separated families; nearly 50 families were briefly reunited. These reunions relieved some of the tension between the North and South.

THE CHILDHOOD OF KIM JONG IL

While Kim was rising as the leader of North Korea, his first son—Kim Jong Il—was growing up. The younger Kim was born during his parents' stay in the Soviet Union on February 16, 1942. At age three, he returned to Korea with his mother, Kim Jong

Suk. He was the oldest of three children, two boys and a girl (Kim Kyong-hee).

Kim Jong Il came to Korea during its rebirth. As a toddler, he did not understand the pains of Korea's past, or the struggles that lay ahead. He learned his earliest lessons at his mother's knee. Kim Jong Suk taught her son that faithfulness to his father as leader should be his primary focus in life. This belief came from her years as a Korean revolutionary. Kim Jong Suk illustrated her love for Korea through her untiring work for Kim and her unshakable loyalty to his authority. These examples made a strong impression on Kim Jong Il, even when he was very young.

As a child, Kim Jong Il toured the countryside with his mother, visiting factories and farms. Young Kim was struck by the grueling labor of the peasants. He witnessed children with sores on their hands and feet who performed hard labor with the adults. When he asked his mother why the people had such difficult lives, she explained that his father—the general—was working to set up a government that would help the working people.

At a young age, Kim Jong Il learned to deal with death and loss. When he was five years old, his younger brother, Shura, drowned in a swimming accident. Two years later, his mother died while in labor. On September 22, 1949, Kim Jong Suk kissed her son good-bye as she left for the hospital. She never returned home. Kim bitterly grieved his mother's death. Losing two family members by the age of seven must have been difficult. Not long after his mother's death, Kim's world was again turned upside down with the start of the Korean War. During the war, Kim Jong Il and Kim Kyong-hee fled Korea into northeastern China.

Like his father, the younger Kim was shuffled about as a child, often changing schools. He began his education before the war at Namsan Elementary School in Pyongyang. While in China, he attended Mangyong-dae School for Children of

Kim Jong Il, in a photograph from the 1950s. Like his father, he moved frequently as a child. He began schooling in Pyongyang, was sent to China during the Korean War, and returned to Pyongyang after it was over.

Revolutionaries. This school was established for the children of high-ranking refugees. In November 1952, Kim transferred to Mangyong-dae Revolutionary School. Here, he attended nine months of classes on ideological and military training. Kim returned home after the truce agreement between the Communist troops and the United Nations Command in August 1953. Since most schools in Pyongyang had been destroyed during the war, Kim enrolled in Samsok Primary School on the outskirts of the city. Later, he transferred to the new Fourth Primary School.

During his middle school days, Kim visited many of the revolutionary sites where his father fought with the Chinese guerrilla army. Growing up, Kim often complained about spending his childhood alone. His father was far too busy with affairs of the state to devote much-needed attention to Kim. Probably for this reason, Kim's behavior as a child was often disruptive. Childhood friends described him as a show-off who was mischievous and stubborn. On more than one occasion, Kim engaged in wild and risky stunts. After middle school, Kim attended First Junior High. During part of his high school years, Kim studied abroad in East Germany and Romania. He graduated from Namsan Senior High in July 1960.

JOINING THE WORKERS' PARTY

Kim Il Sung wanted to train his son in the military rather than in politics. After the younger Kim's graduation, Kim enrolled his son in the Air Force Officers' School in East Germany as a regular cadet. Some historians believe that Kim was emulating Stalin, whose son, Vasily, graduated from the Air Force Academy and later became air force commander of the Moscow district. Aside from this, Kim had many reasons to encourage his son to be an air force officer. During the Korean War, Kim's army suffered from the lack of a skilled air force command. Sending his son to the Air Force Officers'

School was probably part of Kim's underlying desire to build a strong air force.

After only several months at the Air Force Officers' School, the younger Kim withdrew and returned home to Pyongyang. Apparently, he was not fond of the school's harsh discipline and refused to continue. Kim Jong Il turned down other offers to attend reputable colleges and universities in other Communist countries, insisting instead on enrolling in a Korean college. In September 1960, he entered Kim Il Sung University, where he studied political economy. He wrote his thesis on the role of rural counties in building socialism and graduated on May 18, 1964. After Kim Jong Il's graduation, Kim Il Sung appointed his son to the Department of Organization and Guidance of the Central Committee.

While Kim was attending college in 1963, his father remarried, to a woman named Kim Sŏng-ae. Kim Il Sung appointed his new wife to the Democratic Women's Union and later to other government offices, including the Central Committee of the party and the Standing Committee of the Supreme People's Assembly. Idolizing his mother's memory, the younger Kim was not overly warm toward his stepmother.

After being granted a government office, the younger Kim's first order of business was to honor his mother. For years, the public had regarded Kim Jong Suk simply as a partisan who fought alongside Kim Il Sung. She was never even publicly recognized as the first lady of North Korea. In September 1974, a major North Korean Communist periodical ran a feature article on Kim Jong Suk, hailing her faithfulness to the great leader Kim Il Sung. A museum was dedicated to her in her hometown, Hoeryŏng, Hamgŏng pukto. Kim Il Sung's new wife praised Kim Jong Suk as a strong revolutionary and a forerunner of the Korean women's movement.

As a member of the Department of Organization and Guidance of the Central Committee, Kim Jong Il focused his attention on the film industry. Throughout the 1970s, he

Kim Jong Il focused his attention on North Korea's film industry. During the 1970s, he produced six films and musicals. To try to boost interest in the film industry, he had an actress and a director from South Korea kidnapped in 1978.

dabbled in filmmaking and the production of stage plays, producing six major films and musicals. They included *Sea of Blood, Fate of a Member of the Self-Defense Corps, Tell the Story O Forest, Flower Girl, True Daughter of the Party,* and *The Song of Mount Kŭmgang.* Kim even wrote the libretto for some of his musicals.

Kim also allegedly wrote many theoretical theses that received praise for their depth and insight. Among the works are "On Establishing Revolutionary Discipline for Learning Among Students" (1961), "On Characteristics and Invasional Nature of Modern Imperialism" (1962), and "Let Us Thoroughly Protect the Party's Self-Reliant Policy Line to Achieve National Economic Construction" (1965).

The younger Kim also devoted much time to studying theater and literature, and formed relationships with North Korean artists and others in the performing arts. All of his work has been immortalized by the North Korean people. He is considered a cultural authority and a great thinker.

9

The Rising Nuclear Issue

Currently, the issue at the forefront regarding North Korea is the unmonitored development of nuclear weapons. North Korea's obsession with nuclear weapons stems back to the Korean War. With American troops stationed in South Korea, Kim Il Sung constantly felt a threat of invasion. He was also aware that the United States had atomic bombs in the South. Kim wanted to be able to develop his own weapons for military defense. To do this he needed to have intelligence in nuclear research. His greatest chances of obtaining technology would be from China or the Soviet Union.

After the Korean War, in 1956, North Korea and the Soviet Union signed two agreements on nuclear research. A group of North Korean scientists then traveled to the Dubna Nuclear Research Center near Moscow for education and training in nuclear sciences. The Soviet Union also supplied North Korea with a small experimental nuclear

A file picture released by the Korean News Service shows the launching of a multistage rocket in August 1998. North Korea claimed that the rocket carried its first satellite.

reactor, which was placed at Yongbyon during the 1960s. The Soviets insisted that the reactor be inspected regularly by the International Atomic Energy Agency, to ensure that it was not used to convert material to weapons. In this way, the Soviet Union granted assistance to North Korea in nuclear research but limited it to civilian use.

It was not until 1964 that China detonated its first atomic blast. After this successful test, Kim quickly turned to the Chinese in his quest for nuclear weapons. He sent a delegation to Beijing to request assistance in a similar experimental program for North Korea. In a letter to Mao Zedong, Kim cited the brotherhood of the two countries that had spent years of "shared fighting and dying on the battlefield." He felt China and Korea should also share the "atomic secret."

However, Chinese leaders declined Kim's request. They believed the project was too expensive for a small country. Despite this rejection, Kim did not give up on his desire to possess nuclear weapons. Again in 1974, Kim asked for China's assistance, this time because he learned that South Korea was beginning a nuclear weapons program. As had happened earlier, Kim's appeal was denied.

CLANDESTINE PROGRAM YIELDS CRISIS

In the late 1970s, Kim authorized the North Korea Academy of Sciences, the army, and the Ministry of Public Services to begin establishing an independent nuclear weapons program. At this cue, he began expanding the nuclear facilities at Yongbyon. The North Koreans often downplayed their interest in nuclear research, citing power shortages as their main interest in nuclear science. At one point, however, a North Korean official frankly stated, "We need the atom bomb."

North Korea's weapons program was completely self-reliant and operated under extreme secrecy. Not even Kim's close allies—the Soviet Union and China—were allowed to visit the main facilities after the program began. The North Koreans were unaware that their project was not completely clandestine, as the United States was closely monitoring the activity at Yongbyon through satellite pictures.

In 1984, Kim asked the Soviet Union for several civil nuclear power stations because of frequent power shortages. The Soviet Union agreed to supply four light-water nuclear power reactors in December 1985, on the condition that North Korea sign the Nuclear Non-Proliferation Treaty (NPT). Kim agreed to the terms, and North Korea joined the NPT on December 12. Under the treaty, North Korea had 18 months to negotiate and sign an inspection agreement with the International Atomic Energy Agency (IAEA), which conducted routine inspections of all nuclear power facilities. A mistake by the IAEA allowed North Korea an extra 18 months to come up with an agreement, but the deadline passed in December 1988 with no initiative taken by Kim. By this time, North Korea's chances of obtaining the Soviet reactors—the reason it had joined the NPT in the first place—was in serious question, because of its waning relationship with the Soviet Union. At the same time, withdrawing from the pact would cause international commotion.

However, international concerns were already mounting. The United States had been watching the large-scale development at Yongbyon for more than six years, and American intelligence seriously doubted North Korea's claim that it was using the nuclear facilities as a power source. If the North Koreans had the capability to create nuclear weapons, it would be a threat to international security. A North Korean bomb could incite a nuclear conflict involving South Korea and Japan. More dangerous still, nuclear weapons could be sold to countries in the Middle East, where they could fall into the hands of terrorists.

To North Korea, the more the outside world felt threatened by its nuclear program, the more valuable it was to the country. As relations with the Soviet Union and China declined, North Korea had few valuable resources. Kim saw that nuclear weapons could be used as a bargaining chip.

The IAEA continued to pressure Kim to comply with inspection requirements. In response, he refused to allow inspections as long as American nuclear weapons were based in South Korea. By 1989, only about 100 warheads were being stored at Kunsan air base on the west coast of South Korea. The weapons were mainly gravity bombs and artillery warheads.

Spent nuclear fuel rods, kept in a cooling pond, at the nuclear facilities in Yongbyon, North Korea. American intelligence doubted North Korea's claim that the facilities were being used just to generate electrical power.

American military commanders felt it was unnecessary for the bombs to remain in Korea. After extensive debate, the United States gradually began reducing the number of nuclear weapons. This action opened the door for possible negotiations with North Korea for both reconciliation with the South and cooperation with IAEA inspections. By December 1991, the last nuclear warheads were removed from South Korea.

Some amazing steps toward a peaceful North-South relationship took place in December 1991. Both sides adopted the Agreement on Reconciliation, Nonaggression and Exchanges and Cooperation between the South and the North. The agreement was the closest either side had ever come to accepting each other's regime as a legitimate government. The guidelines of the policy were as follows:

- Mutual recognition of each other's systems, and an end to interference, vilification, and subversion of each other.

- Mutual efforts to transform the present state of armistice into a solid state of peace, with continued observance of the armistice until this was accomplished.

- Nonuse of force against each other, and implementation of confidence-building measures and large-scale arms reductions.

- Economic, cultural, and scientific exchanges, free correspondence between divided families, and the reopening of roads and railroads that had been severed at the North-South dividing line.

North Korea refused to discuss its nuclear program in this pact but agreed to meet to develop an agreement on the nuclear issue by the end of the year. The Central Committee of the North Korean Workers' Party held an important meeting on December 24. During the meeting, Kim Jong Il was named supreme commander of North Korea's armed forces. The consensus of the meeting also granted permission for international inspection of the nuclear program and for a nuclear accord with the South. The bilateral negotiations began on December 26. Under the deal, the South agreed to cancel the 1992 United States–South Korea Team Spirit military maneuvers, an exercise in which South Korean troops practiced for the use of nuclear weapons. The military exercises began in 1976 and had been highly criticized by the North Koreans, who claimed the maneuvers were part of preparations for an invasion. Also in the agreement, both sides vowed not to "test, manufacture, produce, receive, possess, store, deploy or use nuclear weapons" and not to "possess nuclear reprocessing and uranium enrichment facilities." In addition to these provisions, the North and South allowed for the other side to inspect their facilities. On December 31, the agreement was signed into effect. Kim Il Sung viewed the nuclear pact as a monumental victory.

Kim Jong Il, center, accompanied by military staff members, inspects the Kim Hyong Jik military medical university of the Korean People's Army.

In 1992, General Hans Blix, the IAEA director, led a team on a six-day visit to North Korea to prepare for a full-scale inspection of the facility at Yongbyon. During the tour, Blix had two surprises. First, the largest building on the site—six stories high and the length of two football fields—was only about 80 percent complete. The other unexpected discovery was that the equipment inside was only about 40 percent ready for production. Blix described the equipment as "primitive" and a long time from being ready to produce the amount of plutonium necessary for a hoard of nuclear weapons. According to the North Koreans, only 90 grams of plutonium (about three ounces) had been produced—on an experimental basis. This amount falls drastically short of the 8 to 16 pounds (3.6 to 7.2 kilograms) required to produce a weapon. However, some suspicion arose as to whether the North Koreans had actually produced more and then hidden it.

The inspectors conducted some tests on the equipment and brought back samples from the tanks to make sure the North Koreans were, in fact, telling the truth. The results indicated that plutonium separation could have taken place on three occasions, as opposed to the isolated operation the North Koreans claimed. Another sophisticated test proved that the sample given to Blix did not match the waste product left in the tank. From these tests, the IAEA concluded that there must be more plutonium, but how much more was not known.

Kim drastically underestimated the capabilities of the IAEA inspectors. What had started out as hope for improved relations led to suspicion, mistrust, and eventually, crisis. The IAEA asked to inspect two sites at Yongbyon that had not been previously declared nuclear-related. One of the buildings was a two-story structure that had been partially covered with landscaping to look like a one-story building. When the inspectors arrived, the North Koreans claimed that the lower floor did not exist. What they did not know, however, was that American satellite photos had showed the North Koreans uncovering and then recovering the lower story in between inspections, and the IAEA was made aware of this fact. The upper floor was filled with heavy weapons, such as tanks and missiles. The North Koreans refused to permit a full inspection, claiming the building was a military unit and therefore exempt from the agreement. The IAEA demanded that North Korea declare the two sites nuclear-related facilities and allow an inspection. Kim's representatives refused.

On February 22, 1993, Blix and other IAEA members met with North Korean delegates to discuss the issue. At the meeting, IAEA representatives presented a dozen satellite photographs of the facility at Yongbyon, exposing the deceptive measures taken by the North Koreans. Upon first reaction, the North Koreans claimed the photographs were fake. At the end of the meeting, the board demanded that the North Koreans allow inspection of the two suspect units immediately. If Kim refused to act, the IAEA would present the issue to the UN Security Council.

North Korea had been accused of cheating, with evidence to support the accusation. The respect of the country and its leaders was at stake. If Kim allowed the inspections, the IAEA would no doubt find evidence that North Korea had initially failed to tell the whole truth, and had tried to cover up its lie. Kim believed it was better to refuse the inspections then lose all credibility as a leader.

In response to the standoff, America reinstated the Team Spirit exercise and scheduled a kickoff for March 9. The day before the exercise, Kim Jong Il ordered the entire nation and armed forces to assume a state of readiness for possible war. In Pyongyang, armored cars surrounded security headquarters and armed police crowded the streets. Civilians were instructed to dig trenches near their homes for protection against air attacks. Once again, North Korea refused to allow inspections, this time claiming that the country was in a "state of semi-war." Blix did not accept this excuse and again demanded that Kim allow the inspections. On March 12, North Korea withdrew from the Nuclear Non-Proliferation Treaty—using the Team Spirit exercise as the primary reason. With this action, North Korea made a nonverbal statement to the world that it was determined to continue its nuclear weapons program.

Implications of North Korea's withdrawal were threefold: A possibility existed that North Korea would, in fact, produce nuclear weapons; the United States and other countries might react so strongly that war would break out on the Korean Peninsula; and the North Koreans expected South Korea to determine to develop a bomb program equal to that of the North. The third implication could start an arms race in Japan and South Korea, destroying international nonproliferation.

North Korea agreed to direct negotiations with the United States. The main objective was to reach a serious bilateral agreement. The first meeting ended in a stalemate, with the most significant accomplishment being an agreement to hold another meeting. In July 1993, just before the second round of

U.S. President Bill Clinton, at the border in South Korea in July 1993, looking into North Korea. During the visit, he said, "It is pointless for [North Koreans] to try to develop nuclear weapons because if they ever use them it would be the end of their country."

negotiations, U.S. President Bill Clinton visited South Korea. During his stay, Clinton visited the Bridge of No Return on the North Korean border. Clinton addressed the press, saying, "It is pointless for [North Koreans] to try to develop nuclear weapons because if they ever use them it would be the end of their country." The statement quickly made its way to Pyongyang, and when negotiations convened on July 14 in Geneva, Clinton's words caused quite a stir. Kim's senior deputy, Kang Sok Ju, attacked the United States for not keeping its promise not to threaten North Korea. Despite his anger, however, Kang did not break off the talks.

At the beginning of the negotiations, Kang reasserted that North Korea's nuclear program had peaceful intentions—to supply the country with energy, not to build weapons. He acknowledged the concern that the large facility had potential for weapons production. In response, Kang suggested that North Korea was willing to replace its entire development program with light-water reactors to meet its energy needs more effectively. North Korea would make this shift if the reactors were supplied by the United States and other countries.

Although light-water reactors would increase North Korea's energy capacities by leaps and bounds, they cost $1 billion each. American energy experts argued that North Korea's energy supply could be attained much more easily and less expensively through non-nuclear means. At the end of the negotiations, the United States agreed to explore with North Korea ways to obtain light-water reactors. This statement was far removed from any promise to do so, though. The talks therefore ended with little progress.

Meanwhile, the North Koreans agreed to allow IAEA inspectors to replace film and batteries in the monitoring equipment at Yongbyon and to perform routine tests. The IAEA objected to this compromise, declaring that North Korea should comply with all demands. Nonetheless, the agency cooperated.

Tensions between the United States and North Korea escalated in January 1994. The Reverend Billy Graham visited North Korea—a trip on behalf of his wife, who as a child lived in Pyongyang with her missionary parents. Graham brought with him a message for Kim from Clinton. Clinton's message simply stated that Kim must cooperate on the nuclear issue in order for relations to improve. The statement infuriated Kim. "Pressure and threat cannot work on us," Kim shouted as he shook his fist in the air.

The nuclear situation heated up to a full boil by the spring of 1994. In March, the IAEA called its inspectors home, and because North Korea had failed to comply with demands, it turned the matter over to the United Nations Security Council. In addition, South Korea again planned to hold its annual Team Spirit exercise, which always brought fierce opposition from the North. During a final meeting between the North and South, North Korean negotiator Park Yong Su threatened South negotiator Song Young Dae, saying, "Seoul is not that far from here. If a war breaks out, it will be a sea of fire. Mr. Song, it will probably be difficult for you to survive."

ECONOMIC CRISIS MOUNTS

In December 1993, at the end of the current seven-year economic plan, the Workers' Party Central Committee announced that North Korea had fallen seriously short of the plan's major goals. In fact, the North's economy was a mere one-sixteenth the size of the South's. Rising successor Kim Jong Il approved a new three-year plan, which took the emphasis off heavy industry and returned it to light industry, foreign trade, and agriculture. The economic shift was a matter of survival. North Korea was unable to feed and clothe its people, placing a tremendous hardship on the public. Kim Il Sung assured the people that they would soon "eat rice and meat soup, wear silk clothes and live in a tile-roofed house." He admitted that, in the previous seven years, North Korea had experienced unforeseen obstacles. With this, Kim closed the door on his economic tradition and approved the new plan.

10

The Nuclear Showdown

I n 1994, the tension between North Korea and the rest of the world intensified. The United States and its allies urged the UN Security Council to pass sanctions—trade boycotts—against North Korea. North Korea insisted that "sanctions are a declaration of war." As the pressure built, the United States dispatched military reinforcements to Asian countries.

The showdown grew out of an issue regarding unloading the irradiated fuel rods from the reactor at Yongbyon. If inspectors were allowed to test the rods, they could determine how many fuel rods had been removed, thus estimating the amount of plutonium previously produced. The North Koreans agreed to allow inspectors to watch them unload the reactor, but refused to let them test the rods. Once a substantial number of rods were removed, the verifiable operating history of the reactor would be lost. By June 2, more than

Hans Blix, the director of the International Atomic Energy Agency, during a news conference in 1994 after he had given a "disturbing" report to the United Nations Security Council about North Korea's refusal to allow full inspection of its nuclear facilities.

60 percent of the fuel rods had been removed. Blix sent a letter to the UN Security Council, stating that the agency could no longer accurately determine the reactor's history. He declared the situation "irreversible." The letter prompted serious discussion for UN sanctions against North Korea.

Kim Il Sung firmly believed he was acting with logic. He explained, "Please compare us to a man: They want us to take off our shirt, our coat, and now our trousers. . . . What they want us to be is a man without defense secrets, just a naked man. We cannot accept that. We would rather accept a war."

In June 1994, Selig Harrison—a U.S. international peace delegate—visited Pyongyang with a new objective: to persuade North Korea to freeze further developments at the reprocessing plants. His approach was to persuade North Korea to halt its nuclear program when binding commitments were made for obtaining light-water reactors. On June 9, Harrison presented his idea to Kim Il Sung. The concept was new to Kim, and he discussed it at length with his negotiator. He then looked at Harrison and said, "This is a good idea. We can definitely accept it if the United States really makes a firm commitment we can trust." Kim also went on to reiterate his denial that North Korea possessed nuclear weapons. "It gives me a headache when people demand to see something we don't have," he said. "It's like dogs barking at the moon."

The United States sent former President Jimmy Carter to North Korea to negotiate a deal with Kim Il Sung. For Kim, Carter's visit was long awaited. Carter was the most prominent American ever to visit North Korea, and his visit brought a successful end to Kim's vigilant effort to make direct contact with American leaders. Kim greeted Carter with a wide smile and a firm handshake.

During talks, Kim explained to Carter that he was frustrated by the distrust of the Americans when he repeatedly declared that North Korea had no nuclear weapons. He asserted that North Korea's interest was in nuclear energy—not weapons. If the United States agreed to help him obtain light-water reactors, Kim promised to dismantle the obsolete gas-graphite reactor and reinstate the Non-Proliferation Treaty. In addition, Kim wanted a guarantee from Washington that the United States would not launch a nuclear attack against North Korea.

In return, Carter made two requests: that Kim temporarily freeze his nuclear program until after the third round of U.S.–North Korea negotiations, and that the two remaining IAEA inspectors who were scheduled to be expelled from North Korea be allowed to stay at Yongbyon. Kim agreed to these conditions. After talks with Washington, Carter requested a third provision: North Korea must agree not to place new fuel rods in the old reactor and not to reprocess rods that had been removed. Eager to end a potentially dangerous crisis, Kim granted the third request.

In celebration, Kim invited Carter to a party on the Taedong River aboard his yacht. The occasion turned out to be a measurable success. As Kim sat across a small table from Carter, the two men discussed issues on North-South relations. Kim expressed his eagerness for "national kinship" and said he would be willing to meet with leaders from the South.

DEATH OF THE GREAT LEADER

On July 7, Kim traveled to his villa in the Myohyang Mountains (Mountains of Delicate Fragrance)—his favorite escape from the summer heat. On the way, he made an on-the-spot inspection of a collective farm. With the scorching midday sun beating down, Kim walked about the farm. When he arrived at his villa, Kim inspected the bathrooms and bedrooms, as he planned to have the South Korean president stay there as a guest. After dinner, Kim complained of being tired. Spending the day in 100°F (37.8°C) heat turned out to be too much for the 82-year-old leader. He collapsed with a massive heart attack.

Doctors were quickly called to the villa, but heavy rains prohibited helicopter flights to the remote residence. The muddy dirt roads made land travel difficult, and precious time elapsed before doctors arrived. When the doctors saw Kim lying lifeless on the floor, they opened up his chest in hopes of restarting his heart. Their efforts proved useless; the Great Leader had died. Kim Il Sung was pronounced dead at 2:00 A.M. on July 8, 1994.

North Korean leaders kept Kim's death a secret from the people for 34 hours. They wanted to make proper arrangements for the first succession. On July 9, news of the president's death was finally announced. A television statement was aired at noon, and many people watched in shock as the announcer relayed the report.

At the funeral, Kim Jong Il sat apart from the other mourners, wearing a dark suit, a mourner's armband, and a perplexed expression. He said nothing about his father—the Great Leader, his loss, or his plans for the country in the midst of its sorrow. In many ways, Kim Jong Il differed from his father. Kim Il Sung grew up in a despairing Korea, was a guerrilla fighter, had founded the state, and stood as an ambitious, determined, and charismatic figure even through his final days. Kim Jong Il had lived the childhood of a prince, given every luxury and opportunity. Until he became supreme commander of the People's Army, he never served a day in the military. Even today, the younger Kim abhors crowds and designates an announcer to read all of his pronouncements. At the time of the Great Leader's death, the survival of the country hinged on this successor, who had been named decades before.

Stories abound about Kim's loose lifestyle of drinking, lavish spending, and womanizing. In 1966, Kim married Hong Il-chon, his college sweetheart. The couple had a daughter together before divorcing in 1971. Shortly afterward, Kim began a relationship with a typist at the Workers' Party headquarters—Kim Yong-Suk. The two were married in 1973.

Over the years, a number of violent acts have been attributed to Kim. The best documented was the kidnapping of South Korean actress Choi Eun Hee and her former husband and film director, Shin Sang Ok. The two were kidnapped separately in Hong Kong in 1978 and brought to North Korea at Kim's request. Kim wanted them in

Pyongyang to improve the film industry. Talking about the kidnapping, Kim boasted, "I just said, 'I need these two people, so bring them here,' so my comrades just carried out the operation." In interviews after their escape, Choi and Shin described Kim as "confident, bright, temperamental, quirky, and very much in charge of governmental as well as theatrical affairs." Kim was also believed to be at the root of the Rangoon terrorist bombing in 1983. In 1987, Kim Hyon Hui, a female North Korean agent, planted a bomb on Korean Air Lines Flight 858 that killed 115 people. Kim Hyon Hui later told authorities that her orders came directly from Kim.

At the same time, Kim's youth did bring about a few favorable changes. He is credited for helping to modernize the country by permitting fashionable clothing and reintroducing cards, dice, and board games.

In the years that preceded Kim Jong Il's succession, North Korean authorities went to great measures to promote his image. His portrait adorns every home, office, and workplace. His name is associated with dozens of North Korean hospitals, which Kim sponsors in honor of his mother's memory. However, these gestures did not earn Kim Jong Il the same adoration or respect the people had had for his father.

Radio announcements in 1994 referred to Kim Jong Il as "the Dear Leader, the sole successor to the Great Leader." The North Koreans thought Kim would assume his father's titles of general secretary and Workers' Party president after the customary 100 days of mourning. After Kim Il Sung's death, though, a power struggle ensued between senior ideologue Hwang Jang Yop and the younger Kim. Hwang eventually fled to South Korea in February 1997. At this time, Kim stepped up and assumed his father's titles. The following year, Kim extended his role as head of the armed forces to include the powers of head of state. He then resigned the post of president, granting it "eternally" to Kim Il Sung.

More than one million people gathered on Kim Il Sung Square in Pyongyang on January 11, 2003, to hear political leaders hail the country's decision to withdraw from the Nuclear Non-Proliferation Treaty. The banners depict Kim Il Sung and Kim Jong Il.

A FORMAL FREEZE

The death of Kim Il Sung did not interrupt negotiations between North Korea and the United States. Talks resumed on August 5, 1994, in Geneva, Switzerland. While negotiations were under way, North Korea froze its nuclear program—as promised to Carter. In Geneva, it was up to the two delegations to come up with a permanent solution in keeping with the previous agreement. Within a week, negotiators succeeded in completing a rough outline for a formal document, with the primary point being North Korea's agreement to abandon its gas-graphite nuclear facilities in exchange for modern light-water reactor plants. The outline also included the discussion of other items, such as the 8,000 irradiated fuel rods that had been removed earlier that year, the reprocessing facility that could extract enough plutonium from the rods to make four or five nuclear weapons, and the IAEA special inspections of the two suspicious sites at Yongbyon.

The talks produced rapid progress, the IAEA inspections being the prickliest issue. North Korea's chief negotiator, Kang Sok Ju, declared that North Korea would "never" submit to any inspection that infringed on its national sovereignty. U.S. negotiators insisted that the acceptance of the inspections be included in the agreement. During negotiations on October 6, Kang proposed that North Korea be exempt from inspections until 70 to 80 percent of the light-water reactors had been shipped. The proposal was a huge leap toward reaching a mutual agreement.

South Korean President Kim Young Sam was infuriated by the course the negotiations were taking. One problem was that South Korea had to pick up a share of the cost for the light-water reactors. Another was the principle of even making a deal with North Korea. He objected to an agreement, saying, "North Korea faces the danger of imminent political and economic collapse. . . . Any compromise [at this point] with North Korea will only help prolong its survival." Kim Young Sam accused the United States of being naïve in its negotiations and claimed that North Korea could not be trusted.

Nevertheless, on October 21, the Agreed Framework was signed by both sides in Geneva. According to the provisions, the United States would provide North Korea with the

Construction work on a light-water nuclear reactor project in Kumho, North Korea. The project is part of a 1994 agreement, under which a U.S.-led international consortium has agreed to build reactors in exchange for the North's agreement to freeze its suspected nuclear weapons program.

requested light-water reactors by 2003. In return, North Korea would comply with IAEA inspections and dismantle its existing nuclear facilities. In the meantime, the United States agreed to supply North Korea with 500,000 tons of heavy fuel oil to aid energy needs. Also included in the agreement was a promise from North Korea to reengage in a North-South dialogue with the intent of normalizing relations.

NORTH KOREA'S DECLINE

Although idolized as the Great Leader, Kim Il Sung left his son a shaky economy. By January 1995, North Korea had experienced five consecutive years of economic decline, and the future did not look promising. In the midst of economic crisis, a natural disaster struck North Korea. On July 26, 1995, the skies opened up over northern Korea, and rains steadily pounded the country for ten days. By the end of the storm, North Korea had received 23 inches (58 centimeters) of rain—some towns recording a devastating 18 inches (46 centimeters) in a single day. The flood was considered the worst in a century.

When the clouds finally broke, North Korea was shoulder deep in a state of emergency. The destruction of crops in an already starving nation placed the people of North Korea in a desperate situation. Many North Koreans were malnourished, and hungry people scavenged the countryside in search of wild plants and roots. The self-reliant country turned to the world for help. In addition to fuel and medical assistance, Kim Jong Il asked the United Nations for $500 million in flood relief. With little faith that the aid would reach the intended victims, aid-givers demanded and were granted direct access to the flood-stricken areas.

By 1996, North Korea's economic situation had seen little improvement. Deteriorating or flooded coal mines hindered energy production required for industry, forcing many factories to close. With fuel so scarce, most people resorted to traveling by oxcart or bicycle. People lived out their winters in unheated homes, and frequent blackouts plagued cities. Agricultural yields suffered again in 1996 due to a drop in fertilizer production. Grain that was produced could not be transported to areas of need, leaving what was left for rats or waste. From 1995 to 1998, famine claimed the lives of an estimated 2 million North Koreans, and those numbers continue to climb. To survive, many people eat leaves, grasses, tree bark, and other scavenged foods. Others barter food, clothing, and fuel at illegal street markets that

Children suffering from malnutrition in Pyongyang. Flooding in 1995 devastated North Korea's crops. From then until 1998, famine claimed an estimated 2 million lives.

have sprung up. Local authorities have little to say about these activities in such desperate times.

Kim Jong Il has acknowledged the serious hardships his country faces. "The most urgent issue to be solved at present is the grain problem," Kim said in a speech at Kim Il Sung University. "The food problem in this country is creating a state of anarchy." He also claimed responsibility for the country's economic difficulties, recalling the energy his father had spent in giving him economic guidance. Kim recalled, "[He] repeatedly told me that if I got involved in economic work, I would not be able to handle party and army work properly." However, Kim went on to criticize the ineffectiveness of his party organizations.

The United Nations and many individual countries have made generous contributions to humanitarian efforts in North

Korea. In 1997, South Korea supplied 50,000 tons of food to its neighbor. China contributed nearly a million tons of food over a one-year period. The UN World Food Program, using funds from the United States, South Korea, the European Commission, and 18 other nations and nongovernmental organizations, provided 200,000 tons of food to the starving country. In mid-1997, the United Nations donated another 129,000 tons for North Korean children age six and younger.

How long the "socialist paradise" can stand on its collapsing economy is uncertain. Recent actions by Kim Jong Il suggest possible desperation while his regime gasps its last breaths. According to one Korean reporter, "[North Koreans] are going down the tubes. . . . There's no possibility of a soft landing. There's going to be a crash."

Kim Il Sung

1912	On April 15, born Kim Sung Ju to Kim Hyong Jik and Kang Bang Suk in the village of Mangyong-dae.
1919	On March 1, participates in the March First Movement.
1920	Moves to Joong-gang; after about a year, moves to Manchuria.
1921	Attends Paldo-gu Elementary School.
1923	In March, travels alone to Korea to continue school at Changduk Elementary.
1925	Returns to Manchuria in January.
1926	Father (Kim Hyong Jik) dies on June 5; enters Whasung Military Academy.
1927	Attends middle school in Jilin; in April, establishes the Korean Jilin Teens' Association.
1928	Participates in the Jilin-Danhua Railway protest.
1929	Arrested and jailed.
1930	Released from jail; assumes name Kim Il Sung.
1932–1941	Fights with Chinese guerrilla forces; mother (Kang Bang Suk) dies in 1932.
1942	Flees to the Soviet Union for protection; marries Kim Jong Suk; first son, Kim Jong Il, is born on February 16.
1944	Second son, Kim P'yŏng-il, is born.
1945	Returns to Korea; daughter, Kim Kyong-hee, is born.
1947	Son Kim P'yŏng-il dies in a swimming accident.
1948	Democratic People's Republic of Korea (DPRK) is founded; Kim is elected the first premier.
1949	Kim Jong Suk dies in labor.
1950–1953	Korean War is fought.
1955	Delivers speech on *chuch'e* concept.
1956	Authority challenged by the Yanan group.

1963 Marries second wife, Kim Sŏng-ae.

1965 Receives honorary doctorate from Ali Archam Institute for Social Sciences, Indonesia.

1968 North Koreans' first assassination attempt on South Korean President Park Chung Hee.

1972 Elected president under North Korea's new constitution; awarded the Order of Double Hero on his sixtieth birthday.

1975 Visits Romania, Algeria, Mauritania, Bulgaria, and Yugoslavia, and receives second honorary doctorate in Algeria.

1977 Reelected to another term as president.

1979 Begins an independent nuclear program.

1982 Seventieth birthday celebration; unveiling of the Arch of Triumph, Tower of Chuch'e, and the Kim Il Sung stadium, all dedicated to Kim; reelected president.

1983 Rangoon terrorist attack in Burma.

1993 Tension grows over the nuclear facilities at Yongbyon.

1994 Reaches a nuclear agreement with former President Jimmy Carter; agrees to freeze nuclear reactors until negotiations can be made for a bilateral agreement; dies of a massive heart attack on July 8.

Kim Jong Il

1942 Born on February 16 to Kim Il Sung and Kim Jong Suk in the Soviet Union.

1945 Moves to liberated Pyongyang with his mother.

1947 Begins kindergarten at Namsan Elementary; brother, Kim P'yŏng-il, dies in a drowning accident.

1949 On September 22, mother dies giving birth to a stillborn baby.

1950 Moves to China for safety during the Korean War; attends Mangyong-dae School for Children of Revolutionaries.

1952 Transfers to Mangyong-dae Revolutionary School.

1953   Korean War ends; returns to Pyongyang.

1960   Graduates from Namsan Senior High; enrolled in East Germany's Air Force Officers' School; withdraws from Air Force Officers' School and begins attending Kim Il Sung University.

1964   Graduates from Kim Il Sung University on May 18.

1966   Marries Hong Il-chon.

1971   Divorces Hong Il-chon.

1973   Marries second wife, Kim Yong-Suk.

1978   Orchestrates kidnapping of actress Choi Eun Hee and her former husband, Shin Sang Ok.

1983   Involved in the Rangoon terrorist bombing.

1987   Orders Kim Hyon Hui to blow up Korean Air Lines Flight 858, killing 115 people.

1994   Father, Kim Il Sung, dies of a massive heart attack on July 8; signing of the Agreed Framework.

1995   In July, floods devastate North Korea; Kim asks the world for help.

1997   Assumes father Kim Il Sung's titles of general secretary and Workers' Party president.

2003   In February, reactivates North Korea's nuclear reactors; threatens to annul the 1953 Korean War armistice; fires a missile into the Sea of Japan.

2003   On March 2, North Korean fighter jets shadow American reconnaissance plane.

Bong, Baik. *Kim Il Sung Biography*. Beirut, Lebanon: Dar Al-Talia, 1973.

Breen, Michael. *The Koreans: Who They Are, What They Want, Where Their Future Lies*. New York: St. Martin's Press, 1998.

Cumings, Bruce. *Korea's Place in the Sun: A Modern History*. New York: W.W. Norton, 1997.

Duus, Peter. *The Abacus and the Sword: The Japanese Penetration of Korea, 1895–1910*. Berkeley: University of California Press, 1998.

Hunter, Helen-Louise. *Kim Il-Song's North Korea*. Westport, CT: Praeger Publishers, 1999.

Institute for South-North Korean Studies. *The True Story of Kim Jong Il*. Seoul, Korea: Institute for South-North Korea Studies, 1993.

Noland, Marcus. *Avoiding the Apocalypse: The Future of the Two Koreas*. Boulder, CO: Institute for International Economics, 2000.

Oberdorfer, Don. *The Two Koreas: A Contemporary History*. Reading, MA: Addison-Wesley, 1997.

Oh, Kongdan. *North Korea Through the Looking Glass*. Washington, D.C.: Brookings Institution Press, 2000.

Phillips, Douglas A., and Steven C. Levi. *The Pacific Rim Region: Emerging Giant*. Hillside, NJ: Enslow Publishers, 1988.

Su, Choe In. *Kim Jong Il: The People's Leader*. Pyongyang, Korea: Foreign Languages Publishing House, 1983.

Suh, Dae-Sook. *Kim Il Sung: The North Korean Leader*. New York: Columbia University Press, 1988.

Sung, Kim Il. *With the Century: Kim Il Sung Memoirs*. Pan-Pacific Economic Development Association of Korean Nationals, http://www.kimsoft.com/war/w-r-0.htm.

ABOUT THE AUTHOR

RACHEL A. KOESTLER-GRACK has worked with nonfiction books as an editor and writer since 1999. She lives on a hobby farm near Glencoe, Minnesota. During her career, she has worked extensively with historical topics, including the colonial era, the Civil War era, the Great Depression, and the civil rights movement.

ARTHUR M. SCHLESINGER, JR. is the leading American historian of our time. He won the Pulitzer Prize for his book *The Age of Jackson* (1945) and again for a chronicle of the Kennedy administration, *A Thousand Days* (1965), which also won the National Book Award. Professor Schlesinger is the Albert Schweitzer Professor of the Humanities at the City University of New York and has been involved in several other Chelsea House projects, including the series REVOLUTIONARY WAR LEADERS, COLONIAL LEADERS, and YOUR GOVERNMENT.